BONHOEFFER IN A
WORLD COME OF AGE

BONHOEFFER IN A
WORLD COME OF AGE

Essays by
PAUL M. VAN BUREN
PAUL L. LEHMANN
EBERHARD BETHGE
MARIA VON WEDEMEYER-WELLER
JOHN D. GODSEY

With a Foreword by
JOHN C. BENNETT

Edited by
PETER VORKINK, II

FORTRESS PRESS
Philadelphia

Paperback Edition 1968
Fortress Press, Philadelphia

These articles, with the exception of the Foreword, Preface, and Bibliography, originally appeared in the Fall, 1967 issue of the *Union Seminary Quarterly Review* (Vol. XXIII, No. 1), 3401 Broadway, New York, New York 10027.

Library of Congress Catalog Card Number 68–14355

5888H67   Printed in U.S.A.   1–1018

FOREWORD

The presence of Dr. Eberhard Bethge at Union Seminary as the Harry Emerson Fosdick Visiting Professor in 1967 made it natural to arrange a colloquium on the thought of Dietrich Bonhoeffer at which the first three chapters in this book were presented as lectures. Professor van Buren was chosen to represent the recent American response to Bonhoeffer which often makes Bonhoeffer a major stimulus behind the secular theology. Actually Professor van Buren, by his emphasis upon the paradox in Bonhoeffer's thought which forms the title of his essay, steers us away from a one-sided use of Bonhoeffer and he indicates that there is a movement in his own thought away from the limits that he had placed around theology in his widely read and provocative volume, *The Secular Meaning of the Gospel*.

Dr. Bethge is the person who knows most about Bonhoeffer's life and thought. He is the friend to whom most of the letters in *Letters and Papers from Prison* were written. He married Bonhoeffer's niece and it was their child whose baptism figures so prominently in the letters. He has edited the collected works of Bonhoeffer and his definitive life of Bonhoeffer, *Dietrich Bonhoeffer,* will soon be published in this country. Professor Paul Lehmann was one of Bonhoeffer's closest friends. They had been contemporaries at Union Seminary in 1931 and Professor Lehmann was very much involved in Bonhoeffer's discussion of his fateful decision to return to Germany in 1939, interrupting his plan to spend a second year at Union Seminary.

It is extraordinary but true that Bonhoeffer is the theologian most influential among the members of the younger generation. He speaks to them, especially in his latest and most radical thought, as no living contemporary seems to do. Readers will quickly note that neither Eberhard Bethge nor Paul Lehmann supports some of the popular uses of Bonhoeffer based upon interpretations of the phrases, "religionless Christianity" and "man come of age," which have made him the inspiration for forms of theology that emphasize the secular and the independence of man so much that the distinctive contributions of Christianity to the world may be lost. Bonhoeffer, in his last years, did become a radical thinker and he saw the problems that may cause many of his contemporary admirers to be more radical than he, but his Christology, apart from anything else, kept him from losing the Christian substance in identifying himself with the world. He brings no comfort to churchmen who seek to preserve the status quo in the church. In Dr. Bethge's second chapter, "Turning Points in Bonhoeffer's Life and Thought," there is much illumination on Bonhoeffer's turning in his thought from the church to the world as he came to concentrate on the political opposition to Hitler which led to his martyrdom. It is a mark of what he turned away from in the church that after his death it was common for churchmen to deny him a role as a Christian martyr because the context of the events leading to his death was political.

We are very grateful to be able to include this second essay by Dr. Bethge and the essay by Professor Godsey which were not part of the program of the colloquium. It is, furthermore, an event of great interest to be able for the first time to present in this volume some of the remembrances of Maria von Wedemeyer-Weller who was Bonhoeffer's fiancée. We are grateful to Mrs. Weller for her willingness to add an important chapter to our knowledge of Bonhoeffer the man.

We also want to thank Peter Vorkink, II, who has worked very closely with Dr. Bethge, for, as editor, rendering valuable editorial assistance in the development of the book and for preparing a most useful bibliography.

There is an enormous amount of literature about Bonhoeffer, but I am confident that this little volume will have a place of its own in that literature because it deals concisely with the most vital problems of interpretation and because four of its essays reflect the most intimate, first-hand knowledge of Bonhoeffer that is now available.

JOHN C. BENNETT

Union Theological Seminary
New York, New York
January, 1968

PREFACE

Interpretations of the life and thought of Dietrich Bonhoeffer are like the answers elicited by a Rorschach test—no two commentators see the same things. Bultmannians view his work as the creative application of demythologization; Tillichians discover that "the world come of age" has affinities to a "theonomous culture"; Barthians, despite Bonhoeffer's criticism of "revelational positivism," find in his thought the extension of the master's critique of "religion"; radical theology locates its *textus classicus* in the *Letters and Papers from Prison;* secularists rejoice in his anti-clericalism; and mass culture finds in his life and death its needed martyr. What Bonhoeffer *really* meant and what he would have said had he lived has become a wide-open pastime, little previous experience required.

The wide diversity in these interpretations indicate that perhaps the boundaries have been overstepped. While some of Bonhoeffer's thought is admittedly incomplete, its interpretation often reveals the views of the interpreter rather than those of Bonhoeffer himself. Even a passing acquaintance with him, however, shows that it is nearly impossible for any one theologian to be the advocate of so many, and at times self-contradictory, positions.

The solution to what is rapidly becoming an impasse in the interpretation of Bonhoeffer lies not in proof-texting specific theological positions, but, rather, in a return both to the times in which he lived and to the issues with which he was wrestling in his own theological development, with special emphasis on the biographical aspect of his theological affirmations. While there is uncertainty where Bonhoeffer's thinking might have evolved had he lived, there is a consensus developing among scholars concerning the decisive question about which his life and work centered, viz., the concrete presence of Christ; all else is subsumed under this. Whether the question is "Who is Christ?" (which is the governing idea up until the church struggle) or whether it is the same phrase with "today" introduced into it (which denotes what is really "new" in the letters from prison) it remains the same issue. While the question was forever in his thought, Bonhoeffer found he had several answers to the one question. The answers, however, were not developed successively, one theme after another; rather, they are to be seen as leitmotifs, constantly reoccurring as they weave in and out of the dynamism of Bonhoeffer's thought. Each in its own way has its intrinsic meaning, but none can be made to bear the entire weight of his theology. "Non-religious interpretation," "religionless Christianity," "this-worldly transcendence," and "secret discipline" are not programs in themselves but probes into the future as Bonhoeffer attempts to answer his central question.

If Eberhard Bethge is right in his recently published biography in chronicling Bonhoeffer's life as a progression from theologian to Christian to contemporary, then there is an even closer connection between Bonhoeffer's actions and his writings than we have hitherto imagined. Just as Bonhoeffer's life might be the translation of some of his enigmatic formulas, so might those catch-words be the clues to our understanding of what it means to be a twentieth-century Christian. The more we are able to straighten out the relationship between Bonhoeffer's life and thought, the closer we will be to providing a clearer understanding of our own situation.

This little volume may prove to be very helpful in exploring the connection between Bonhoeffer the man and Bonhoeffer the theologian because, among other things, three of the contributors warrant special consideration by virtue of their personal relationship to him. Eberhard Bethge was Bonhoeffer's closest friend in Germany, his virtual alter-ego in the last decade of his life. Few know Bonhoeffer's thought and its context as well as Bethge, who has gone on to be his posthumous editor and, most recently, his official biographer. Paul Lehmann was Bonhoeffer's best friend in America, when they were student contemporaries at Union Theological Seminary, and has since become one of the foremost American interpreters of both Bonhoeffer's life and theology. Maria von Wedemeyer-Weller, who became engaged to Bonhoeffer twenty-seven months before his death and who was the recipient of more than forty prison letters, here appears in print for the first time and exposes a side of Bonhoeffer long hidden from the world.

In addition to these four contributions are essays by two other men whose names have long been associated—for differing reasons—with the interpretation of Bonhoeffer. Paul van Buren, once unhappily grouped with the radical theologians, draws upon the writings of William James, Ludwig Wittgenstein, and others in an attempt to straighten out Bonhoeffer's paradoxical language about God. John Godsey, whose continuing interest in Bonhoeffer goes back to his book, *The Theology of Dietrich Bonhoeffer,* presents a precisely documented essay on the injustices done to Bonhoeffer in English translation.

This volume is in no sense the final word, but it is my hope that each essay in its own special way will help to fathom the life and thought of a man who has so fascinated and bedeviled the contemporary theological scene.

PETER VORKINK, II

Union Theological Seminary
New York, New York
December, 1967

ACKNOWLEDGEMENTS

Permission to quote from the following volumes by Dietrich Bonhoeffer has been graciously granted by their respective publishers:

Christ the Center. Translated by John Bowden. New York: Harper & Row, 1966. Copyright ©, 1960, Christian Kaiser Verlag, Munich, in Bonhoeffer's *Gesammelte Schriften*, Vol. 3; Copyright ©, 1966, in the English translation by William Collins Sons & Co., Ltd., London, and Harper & Row, Publishers, Inc., New York.

The Cost of Discipleship. Translated by Reginald H. Fuller. New York: Macmillan, 1963. Second edition ©, SCM Press, Ltd., London, 1959.

Ethics. Edited by Eberhard Bethge and translated by Neville Horton Smith. New York: Macmillan, 1965. Copyright ©, 1955 by The Macmillan Company.

Letters and Papers from Prison. Edited by Eberhard Bethge and translated by Reginald H. Fuller and others. New York: Macmillan, 1967. Third edition, revised and enlarged. Copyright ©, 1953 by The Macmillan Company.

The Way to Freedom. Translated by Edwin H. Robertson and John Bowden. New York: Harper & Row, 1966. Copyright ©, 1958–61, by Christian Kaiser Verlag, Munich, in Bonhoeffer's *Gesammelte Schriften*, Vol. 2; Copyright ©, 1966, in the English translation by William Collins Sons & Co., Ltd., London, and Harper & Row, Publishers, Inc., New York.

All quotations from *Radical Theology and the Death of God*, Copyright ©, 1966 by Thomas J. J. Altizer and William Hamilton, are reprinted by permission of the publishers, The Bobbs-Merrill Company, Inc., Indianapolis.

ABBREVIATIONS

References to works by Bonhoeffer in the essays beginning on pages 46 and 73 have been abbreviated as follows:

GS   *Gesammelte Schriften*, Vols. I-IV

WF   *The Way to Freedom*

CC   *Christ the Center*

CD   *The Cost of Discipleship* (paperback, 1963)

E   *Ethics* (paperback, 1963)

LP   *Letters and Papers from Prison* (3rd edition, 1967)

WE   *Widerstand und Ergebung*, München: Chr. Kaiser Verlag, 1964 (12th edition)

For full information, consult the Bibliography on page 133.

TABLE OF CONTENTS

BONHOEFFER'S PARADOX:
LIVING WITH GOD WITHOUT GOD

A Hypothetical Investigation

by Paul M. van Buren

When people say things of an illogical sort, when they combine contradictory elements in one sentence, we often dismiss them as muddled or stupid. There are cases, however, in which we are inclined to treat illogicalities with more respect, cases in which something about the person, the way he speaks, or the situation leads us to suspect that the illogicality, the paradox, is intentional. Intentional paradoxes are sometimes signals of a discovery, a discovery of a new way of seeing something all too familiar. Some intentional paradoxes serve to shake us loose from old mental habits and lead us to the point at which the speaker stands, from which we may see things in his new way. They invite us to share in a newly discovered view of familiar matters.

I want to explore Dietrich Bonhoeffer's paradoxical language about God in order to see if it is of this sort. If we assume that he was not stupid or talking nonsense, then we shall proceed under the assumption that he may have had something important to say with his paradox, that he may have had a new way of seeing things, or at least a way of seeing things that was new for him. This presumed discovery of Bonhoeffer's, then, shall be our goal, which means that we are looking for a clear view of the way in which Bonhoeffer was looking at things. Our method will be to go behind his paradox, as it were, in order to work through his discovery without feeling obliged to leave it in the words in which he left it—that is, as a paradox. What I shall argue is that his paradox signals a shift in world hypotheses, in root metaphors for understanding life and the world, in short, in metaphysics. Bonhoeffer intended to reject one world hypothesis, one metaphysics. From the fragments remaining from the period in which he developed the paradox which we are to investigate, it is not altogether clear whether he thought, as have so many other theologians, that he was thereby free from involvement in any metaphysics. I think he thought that he was, for there is no evidence that he was aware that to reject one view of things is already to have adopted another view. It is this displacement of hypotheses that seems to me to be the heart of our subject, which is why I have subtitled this paper, "A hypothetical investigation."[1]

The fascinating thing about Bonhoeffer, for many of us in the next generation following him, is that where his theology becomes really interesting, it is preserved in only bits and snatches. One result of this sketchy character of his last ideas is that he has been claimed by the most orthodox and the most radical elements of

[1] My indebtedness for many of the ideas in this paper to the writings of William James, Stephen Pepper, John Wisdom, and Ludwig Wittgenstein will be obvious. Let this general note suffice to indicate this and to excuse them from any responsibility for the ways in which I have interpreted their ideas and the use I have made of them.

contemporary theology. The paradox which I have chosen comes from this last period, and indeed, you can dismiss it altogether, if you want to. On the one hand, it can be discounted as the uncertain, wild talk of a man who less than a year earlier wrote that he was enjoying reading non-theological authors, as though this were quite a new experience for him. Karl Barth discounted Bonhoeffer's last writings in just this way, seeing in them the expression of the trauma of a man who in prison found himself for the first time in his life outside of the relatively narrow context of church and theology in which he had always lived and thought.

One could also discount our paradox on other grounds. It occurs most clearly in a letter dated July 14, 1944, just six days before the attempt on Hitler's life, the failure of which led to Bonhoeffer's own death. Loose and irresponsible language might be expected in such a time of tension. So who is right, the conservatives or the radicals? God knows what Bonhoeffer meant, that is, what he would have said had he lived to develop his ideas or to see what others found themselves saying because of what he wrote. And to that we may add, God knows what we mean when we use that all-too-common expression, "God knows."

In any case, judging Barth to have been guilty of the genetic fallacy, I do not choose to dismiss Bonhoeffer's paradox. At least I want to think a bit about it. So first of all, let us state it in his words: "*Vor und mit Gott leben wir ohne Gott.*" He put it in other words too, but this form will do, for in any case, I want to put the paradox in English, and that in more ways than one.

3

That is to say, I am not primarily interested in Bonhoeffer, but in his paradox, and I mean to investigate it in my way, not his. Literally, the paradox translates, "Before (as it were, in the face of or in the presence of) and with God we live without God." Or, to bring out the paradox a bit more sharply, "We live with God without God," as I put it in my title.

Now when I said I wanted to put that into English, I intended more than just a verbal translation. I meant that I want to explore this paradox as it would be explored in English, which calls for methods of analysis of which Bonhoeffer, as far as I can see, was quite unaware. I mean I want to know what it means, and that means several things. It can mean, I want to see if there is another way of saying the same thing which would not be so liable to draw a blank stare. Or, if "saying the same thing in other words" strikes you as being as problematic and ambiguous an enterprise as it does me, then let us say that I want to see if there is a way to speak that will do for me what this paradoxical sentence in German seems to have done for Bonhoeffer, or at least something related to that. Intellectual honesty, for which Bonhoeffer was also concerned, compels me to say that I cannot hope for more than that. Any way in which we deal with Bonhoeffer's words, or indeed with any other words, involves more or less abstraction. Those words were his, written out of a certain life and in most particular circumstances. Let them stand as they are, part of his own life, speaking for themselves. But we can now proceed to explore our own English paradox which we have abstracted from

4

Bonhoeffer's writings, attempting to set them into our own living context to see how they might come alive. I want to explore this paradox because I think that by doing so we can shed a bit of light on some of our problems in theology today. I hope to make clear that in that light we may be seen to be heading in a direction which was reasonably clearly seen by an American thinker some sixty years ago, an American theologian insufficiently appreciated by most of the theological community, namely, William James. And now to our investigation.

The paradox has two sides, "with God" and "without God." Let me begin with the second or negative part first. And here we run into a problem before we can even begin, for Bonhoeffer's point here is not just negative. The negative is enclosed as it were in a positive: living. "Living without God" is the subject, and that involves first of all living. It seems to have meant at least that we are asked to do what we seem to be required by our circumstances to do in any case: to take full responsibility, unqualified responsibility for working things out on our own, that is, in human terms. This is the positive side of Bonhoeffer's repeated thesis that men do not need God today, that we can and do get along just as well or better without "the God hypothesis" as with it. We cope with life and this world as human beings without recourse to any higher power, some *Deus ex machina,* to help us solve our problems. We may or may not do well, but in any case it is up to us. We do the best we can with what we have at hand:

ourselves. The terms of our problems, our solutions, and our failures are our own, human terms.

But what are human terms? What is it, for Bonhoeffer, to be a man? Clearly the image of man for him was his image of Jesus Christ. To take full responsibility for this world and to work things out in human terms, as Bonhoeffer saw it, was to work things out in terms of the man Jesus, as Bonhoeffer saw that man. In short, the criterion of manhood was that presented in the biblical story, the story of the despised and rejected "man for others." That seems to have been Bonhoeffer's frame of reference. Human terms, did I say? Are there not other than human terms of reference in that story? Does that story not tell us of God? Well, it does in a way, but I gather that Bonhoeffer wanted to emphasize that whatever that story tells us of God, it does so in the human terms provided by the human figure of Jesus Christ. To experience God, he wrote, means to meet Jesus Christ. To be in a relationship to God means to live for others, sharing in that form of life which was Jesus Christ's.

We have, as you see, already passed to the positive side of the paradox, which seems to suggest that we have on our hands only an apparent paradox. For to live with God, "*vor und mit Gott*," is, as we have said already, to meet Jesus Christ, to live a new life of "being for others." Again, the frame of reference is the same: the biblical story of "the man for others."

So far, so good, and no doubt everyone may find comfort from this, fit it into his own theological scheme, and find Bonhoeffer on his side. The difficult problems are not yet exposed. So now we dig deeper, carry the

6

analysis a step further. It was, apparently, an important point for Bonhoeffer that Christian faith did not commit one to what he called repeatedly "the God hypothesis." Indeed, he seems to have almost wanted to say that the Christian should reject the God hypothesis. What was this that he wanted to reject, or that he at least thought was superfluous to Christian faith?

Well, in its broadest terms, the God hypothesis was the theism of Western thought, the theism, for example of Descartes. And what is wrong with the theism of Descartes? Well, perhaps we could say that Descartes' God is too big. And let us not pretend that Descartes stood alone. The God of Descartes, and not only of Descartes, was the God who could do anything, literally do anything in or about this world. He was unambiguously omnipotent. He was prime mover, first cause, the ground of all being, and all the rest. If he wanted to make us think that every square had three sides and led us to count the sides in such a way that we came up with four every time, he could do that too. He was the absolute in all its glory, the Supreme Being raised to the nth degree. In Descartes' terms, Bonhoeffer was an atheist.

Bonhoeffer, I need hardly say, had a God, but it was not the God of Descartes. Bonhoeffer's God was powerful, but it was that odd sort of power that takes the form of weakness. Was he powerful? Well, we find our paradox coming back again, for God's power, according to Bonhoeffer, was in fact the power of powerlessness. He was a weak God, and that is exactly what Bonhoeffer liked about him. We need not state it quite so para-

7

doxically. We may simply say that this God was not omnipotent in any traditional Western sense of the term, and that Bonhoeffer thought there was much to be said for what weakness could accomplish in this world. More questions about this God could be asked, but let us look at the other side of the matter first.

To believe in and rely upon the God of Western theism is to rely on the God hypothesis. Maybe that is not precisely what Bonhoeffer was saying, but let us leave it at that for the moment in order to consider another side of the matter. What sort of hypothesis is this, this God hypothesis? I want to set aside precise questions about this God for the moment and consider hypotheses, opening up this question from a particular angle.

We have many sorts of hypotheses with which we operate. Indeed without hypotheses of a good number of sorts, we could not operate at all. Many of our hypotheses are vague and general, such as the sort we hardly ever formulate for ourselves. We operate on the vague hypotheses that other things being equal, the world we know will go on operating in more or less the same way tomorrow as it did yesterday, that the language we used yesterday will serve us today, that the bread we buy today we shall be able to eat tomorrow. We also have more specific but more restricted hypotheses. We have hypotheses about the flow and distribution of money on which we rely in monetary affairs. We have hypotheses of yet more exact form on which we rely in scientific work. We call these hypotheses, because, although we rely on them, we also test them out by our further experience. We rely on them in so far as they seem to check out, in so far as they serve their purpose and allow us to proceed without confusion or chaos, in so far as with their help we find that we can move through life.

There is also another sort of hypothesis with which we operate, which may be vague for one and specific for another. In so far as the world we experience, the world of money, politics, science, and all the rest, in so far as this is all part of the world we experience, we tend to see this world in one way or another. We have, each of us, whether precise or fuzzy, whether explicit or implicit, a view of the world. There comes a point for any of us at which we find we want to say, "But this is how things are. They just are this way." And if we take the trouble to become aware and articulate about our world views, and if we then attempt to say what they are, what we are doing may also be called metaphysics.

What is metaphysics? Well, the most general answer, I suppose, would be that it is an attempt to describe the structure of our understanding of how things are generally, that is, how the whole is, how everything taken together is. Or to put it in other words, it is an attempt to describe the workings of the language in which we say "this is how things are." I say "describe," but I do not wish to pretend that metaphysicians merely describe what is already seen by all. In a sense, of course, this is exactly what they do, for every metaphysics has been a particular proposal of a way of seeing and therefore of talking about what is before us all the time. But it is also a proposal. Any one metaphysics bids for our agreement, not always there before we hear the proposal, that things are like this, not that. In describing what may be called the structure of our understanding of the world, or what I should prefer to call our way of speaking of the world, a metaphysical system or hypothesis is offering us a particular description which we are asked to accept, and this may call on us to revise our familiar descriptions. In this sense, I should be cautious about drawing a hard and fast line between revisionary and descriptive metaphysics.

A metaphysics is by its character a hypothesis. That is, it is proposed to us as a way to see the world, a way to speak of the world, and the assumption seems to be that we shall find that this checks out with our own experience of the world. Since it is, in one way of defining it, a description or an attempted description of the structure of our understanding of the universe, since it appeals to our understanding, bids to be the key to our understanding, a dogmatic metaphysics is a self-contradiction. Metaphysics is by its own proper role hypothetical, asking to be tested, subject to revision on the basis of further experience. It entails at its heart the critical role of understanding.

Now we take a difficult step: I want to argue at this point that Christian faith, in its traditional forms and expressions has been, or, if you prefer, has implied, a world view of just this sort. That is to say, the believer has found himself at certain points forced to say, "But this is how things are." Moreover, he has had to say this concerning matters central to his understanding of things as a believer. Indeed, it is at just these points, although not only here, of course, that he has spoken of God. Taking metaphysics as I have, as it has been understood increasingly since the revolution through which English-speaking philosophy passed during the second quarter of this century, as an exposition of a way of seeing what is before us all the time, the whole world of our experience, I do not see how we could deny that every Christian theology is in its broad lines a particular metaphysics. It has a view of the whole, of heaven and earth, it has a root metaphor, of a personal God and his creation, and it bids for or assumes our agreement that this is indeed how things are. Not only do I fail to see how one can deny this; I see no reason whatsoever for any theologian wanting to deny this. A so-called biblical theology, of the sort that was in high fashion in the forties and fifties, for example, may wish to have no part of the particular metaphysics of Aristotle or of Plato, or of Descartes for that matter. Of course not, for these are other metaphysics, in competition with the way of saying how things are which was characteristic of that particular twentieth-century metaphysics called biblical theology.

If this view of theology is allowed, if in this contemporary sense it is recognized that a theology is one sort of metaphysics, then it is, as we have argued, a hypothesis. It may be a hypothesis held with profound conviction and great dedication, but it is a hypothesis nonetheless. Its proponent asks us to test and see, even to taste and see whether the world is not as it depicts it. It bids us to test and to think, and when it takes a dogmatic turn (using the word in its pejorative sense), when it rules out the critical role of understanding, it breaks with its own tradition of faith seeking understanding, it turns from the Logos it claims to detect and worship, it becomes something contrary to man rather than for man. In this sense, theology as metaphysics is hypothetical, open to correction, subject to further reflection, criticism, and revision.

If one reflects on the general form of theology as a world hypothesis, as a metaphysics, it is evident that God has been not only a piece of this hypothesis, as theology has on the whole developed in the West. God has been the key figure, and that in a particular way. In any metaphysics, one comes sooner or later to the element or elements which are sometimes called first principles. You can find out which they are by asking, "What must I be able to talk about, in this view of things, in order to talk about the other things?" I think I am being reasonably fair to most Western theology, at least up until modern times, if I say that it has been argued that in order to understand, to talk about man and the world, one must be able to speak of God. That is to say, one speaks of man or the world in terms of, or in their relations to God. Man and the world are God's creatures, and unless we begin speaking of man and the world in that way, the tradition argued, all our further speaking will be false. This is what is involved in saying that in traditional Western theology, God has had ontological priority, or God has been the unique first principle, whether in the theology of Aquinas or in that of Calvin. It means that God is the term of reference for everything else, that we speak of man and the world in reference to God, not the reverse. As a result, speaking of God was in no sense a secondary problem for traditional theology, by no means a problem to be turned over to apologetics or practical theology. On the contrary, for the Western tradition, speaking of God was, we may say, of the very essence of the theological enterprise. Theology was what its name can be read to mean etymologically: language about God, from beginning to end.

By this line of argument, we find traditional theology to be a metaphysics, a world hypothesis in which God is the single first principle, having linguistic or ontological priority. It is not misleading, therefore, to speak of this as a God hypothesis. It is a hypothesis about everything that is, and the central term, logically and linguistically, is God. If you wish to reject this God hypothesis, you may do so, but you may then be asked what you propose to put in its place. As a way of considering that, let us see where we come out with Bonhoeffer's theology when looked at in the light of these considerations.

Bonhoeffer argued that Christian faith does not give us a hypothesis for solving many of the problems with which we are faced. Its hypothesis provides no help in dealing, for example, with problems of physics or astronomy or geology, and this goes rather far toward denying to theology the role of a world hypothesis. We do not first need to speak of God in order to speak of these other matters. That means that in at least these regions of discourse, God does not have ontological priority. Yet for Bonhoeffer, in at least some important regions of human life and language, the story of Jesus Christ, Jesus as "the man for others," the behavior of Jesus within the biblical story as Bonhoeffer read it, was the key to understanding, the first principle, that which he said we must first be able to speak of before we can properly speak of other matters. If not so surely universal in scope as the God hypothesis of the tradition, yet within the range of human ethical, political, and cultural behavior, a Jesus hypothesis, or a Christ hypothesis, is operative in Bonhoeffer's view of things. Moreover, what we mean by the word "God" must be learned from how we speak of Jesus. That is to say, we shall not properly speak of God unless we have first learned to speak of Jesus, and we shall then speak of God in terms of Jesus, not the reverse. Jesus, or more strictly, the behavior of Jesus, Jesus as "the man for others" now displaces God as the root metaphor, now takes the place of ontological priority.

But, it might be objected, was not this ontological priority of Jesus implicit in the doctrine of the Trinity, at least if we see that doctrine through the eyes of Karl Barth? If the God of Christian faith is unqualifiedly the one who makes himself known in Jesus Christ, then was Bonhoeffer saying anything other than what Barth had said? And in that case, is this not still a God hypothesis, specifically the peculiar sort of God hypothesis of Barth's *Dogmatics*? Then are not Bonhoeffer's disparaging remarks about the God hypothesis actually misleading? For on this showing, he was arguing not against every

God hypothesis, but only against one and for another. In which case, the conservatives may lay full claim to Bonhoeffer, whereas the radicals would appear to have misled us by appealing to his last writings.

I am not particularly interested in settling the question of who has the better claim to Bonhoeffer credentials, but it does seem to be overdoing it to claim that Bonhoeffer was arguing for a trinitarian God hypothesis as simply as this objection concludes. Some important discrepancies have been overlooked. Although it may be said that shifting ontological priority from God to Christ is only a tiny move further in the direction in which Barth had already taken a theology of revelation, still it is a step further and an important one. With this little step, although we may continue to speak of God, we are required to speak of God in terms of the first principle, who is, after all, a man. Certainly not "man in himself," Bonhoeffer insisted, whatever that may be, but the man for others. Yet for all that, man, specifically a particular man, is now the first principle, the key to understanding even God, and it is in terms of this man that we are to learn how to speak of God. Is this still within the range of Barth's thought? A relationship between the thought of these men is not to be denied, but I should think one could make a better case for setting Bonhoeffer within another realm of discourse, for understanding him in the light of the thought of one who opposed what I think is the same God hypothesis that Bonhoeffer rejected, the God of rationalism, of classical Western theism, and who did so precisely for the sake of man.

William James, almost forty years before Bonhoeffer, granted that the idea of the omnipotent, absolute God of Western theism had a certain nobility, but then remarked, in words which I think Bonhoeffer would rather have enjoyed, had he ever read them:

> In this real world of sweat and dirt, it seems to me that when a view of things is "noble," that ought to count as a presumption against its truth, and as a philosophic disqualification. The prince of darkness may be a gentleman, as we are told he is, but whatever the God of earth and heaven is, he can surely be no gentleman. His menial services are needed in the dust of our human trails, even more than his dignity is needed in the empyrean.[2]

James never developed an explicitly christological basis for this way of speaking of God, yet the affinity is no less interesting. Formally speaking, the structure of Bonhoeffer's and James' metaphysics do not seem to be so different. In each there is serious language about God, and in each man the sweat and dirt of this real world gives us the terms for speaking of God. In each God is weak and man is called to full responsibility for what is to come of things. Let me illustrate with one more passage from James. Speaking of his idea of the world as unfinished, as growing "piecemeal by the contribution of its several parts," James wrote:

> Take the hypothesis seriously and as a live one. Suppose that the world's author put the case to you before creation, saying: "I am going to make a world not certain to be saved,

[2] William James, *Pragmatism* (Cleveland and New York: World Publishing Co. [Meridian Books], 1955), p. 57.

16

a world the perfection of which shall be conditional merely, the condition being that each several agent does its own 'level best.' I offer you the chance of taking part in such a world. Its safety, you see, is unwarranted. It is a real adventure, with real danger, yet it may win through. It is a social scheme of co-operative work, genuinely to be done. Will you join the procession? Will you trust yourself and trust the other agents enough to face the risk?"[3]

James hoped that we would, for he felt we would see that this is just the world we do in fact live in, a world of risk and danger, in which it matters what we do. Is not this also the risky, dangerous, adventurous world that Bonhoeffer saw, in which God surely fails again and again, in which we gamble on its winning through, but hold no guarantee that it will?

I think I am aware of the ways in which it is silly to think of William James as a theologian. I wish I were as sure that we could agree that it would be simply stupid for us today not to take James seriously in our present attempts to find our way ahead in the theological enterprise. However you may feel about that one, I want to try out the framework on which James was working during his last years, to see how Bonhoeffer's and our problem looks in this new setting. The procedure may be a bit unusual, but the results may be at least entertaining, and possibly even instructive.

What I am suggesting calls upon us to consider the possibilities of the hypothesis of a limited God within a pluralistic universe. Let us take this slowly, a piece at a time. What sort of hypothesis is that of a pluralistic

[3] *Ibid.*, p. 187.

17

universe? Well, as the word "universe" warns us, it is a world hypothesis, an all-inclusive view of things. But as a hypothesis of the structure of the totality of our understandings, it says that we understand the whole by understanding the parts. To know the whole better means nothing other than seeing the different parts more and more clearly in the infinite variety of their interconnections and relationships, in their disparities and disjunctions, as well as in their similarities and connections. The world is one, as James liked to put it, in so far forth as conjunctions pertain, but then not one in so far forth as disjunctions pertain. The universe of our understanding, of our experience, or, I should like to add, of our language, is as it were a cube through which many different lines can and are drawn, going in every sort of direction. Some of the lines are long, going from one side to another; some are short, suspended in thin air, as it were, not touching any side of the cube. Some lines touch none or few of the other lines, some touch many other lines at many points. And of course, for any particular purpose which you may have in mind, you can always insert other lines, make or notice other connections, break some of the connections which you have found.

Such is one model of pluralism, a root metaphor of plurality as a hypothesis of how we actually experience, understand, and speak in and of the world. It does not have any one first principle. It has many principles, and which is first and which second depends on what you are trying to do or understand at the moment. Marx gave us some useful first principles which proved to be helpful in certain areas of our experience and with which it turned out to be possible to draw such different lines as Communist ideology and the discipline of sociology. If social analysis is your aim, here are some first principles at least worth considering. When art history or art criticism is our purpose, however, we have found that Marx is misleading. Here other principles prove to have a better claim to priority. In physics and atomic or subatomic analysis of matter, yet other principles prove their merit. And so it goes. I do not say that there are no ways in which these different parts connect: on the contrary, we can only look and see in each case whether there are such conjunctions and of what sort they are.

I used a cube as an image of this view of our understanding and language, but I think there is something to be said for another image, one related to that which Wittgenstein used in speaking of our language as an old city. The image I want to suggest is that of an actual city. Not, I should add, the so-called secular city, but a real city, say any of our great metropolitan cities, such as New York, with its old sections, its odd corners, its multiple villages, its cross-currents of a financial world and a theater world and a clothing world and an educational world, and including also its slums and its suburbs. Is it one at all? Well, the answer to that depends on the context in which the question is asked. For some purposes and in certain respects, it is one, in a number of different ways, and no one of these ways tells us all we know or want to know, just as no one jargon will be understood right across the board in every situation of human activity taking place in the city. Some agreement in the use of a common language would appear to be pragmatically necessary for life in any city, but each specific life in the city calls also for some degree of mastery of techniques not common to all. If we gain a clear view of the plurality of language as we use it, we shall have gained important insight into the plurality of our experienced world.

Now how are we to think of a limited God within this pluralistic universe? Suppose there is something in the suggestion that in rejecting the God hypothesis, Bonhoeffer, consciously or unconsciously, more implicitly than explicitly, was reflecting a move into a form of life which operates with the hypothesis of pluralism. Perhaps most of us in the West have also made this move by now. Of what do we speak when we speak of God in this modern metaphysical framework? It seems difficult to draw an analogy from any of the particular powers or forces at work in our actual city. Yet there is one way in which some of us speak sometimes in the city which may provide a clue. Some of us some of the time talk about the spirit of the city. We call it a great little town. Or we talk of it as the wicked city. We say that it is dead, or we say that it has a certain atmosphere of excitement, a life of its own, a character. Sometimes we appeal to this spirit or character in setting out to change something about the city or one small piece of it. Maybe we occasionally find we want to say that we see the heart and spirit of this city embodied in a particular person we have met or know of.

For Bonhoeffer, I suggest, there was such a particular person, the man for others. If you have heard his story,

then you have come face to face with what gives life
to the city, what defines the city, from Bonhoeffer's point
of view. This will tell you little or nothing about some of
the regulatory problems of the securities exchange. It
will not help you at all in determining the best method
of mechanical or electronic control of air pollution. It
will not tell you whether a given company could survive
in the city if it switched a number of its operations to a
cybernetic system. The issue of the spirit of the city is
important, but it is not omnipotent.

If, however, the question is one of a vision of what
life might be in the city, if the question is one of "what
it all means," whether it is worthwhile trying to do anything about the mess of the city at all, in so far as this
is a question of what I should do now, whether I should
accept my own responsibility about the problems of the
city, in so far as it is a question of what it means to be
a man, in this city, then what I think about the spirit or
character of the city, whether I care about the spirit of
the city, and concretely, what I find myself using as my
image of what it is to be a man in this city may be the
most important single thing about me.

The image of man which played this important role
for Bonhoeffer was the image he took to be that presented by the New Testament picture of Jesus; but it
was important for Bonhoeffer that we approach the New
Testament from the Old, that Jesus be seen within the
context and against the background of Israel, standing
as the center point, as it were, of the image of man expressed in the Old Testament. But did not the men of
Israel, and the men of the New Testament, and above

all Jesus himself believe in God and speak of God? Of course they did. Yet to ask, "What is God?" (which was the title of the main section of the central chapter of Bonhoeffer's little book, which he never lived to write but which he outlined in one of his last letters), to ask, "What is God?" seems to have been a question which Bonhoeffer found he could answer only indirectly, by speaking of the man for others. It is as if someone were to ask, "But what *is* the spirit of New York?" and the answer were given in the form of telling about the man whom we regarded as the true New Yorker. In so far as Bonhoeffer was moved to speak of God, a man provided him the terms with which to speak. Within the relative priorities of the city, and the priorities will always be relative in a pluralistic view of how things are, a particular view of a particular man, but in any case, a man proves to be prior to even a limited God.

Then why even speak of a limited God? Is this not really a certain sort of humanism, set within a pluralistic metaphysics? Well, let us say it is at least that. Whatever Bonhoeffer ended as, it was at least as a humanist. But now two things need to be added to qualify this humanism properly, and without these qualifications, it would be misleading to call Bonhoeffer a humanist. First, this particular humanism influences even the model of plurality, leading us to think, for example, of a city rather than of a cube, more adequately developed with the model of a human city than with that of an impersonal cube. It leads us to speak rather anthropomorphically of the city, of its spirit, its character, its pain and suffering, its joys and its life. We would not have caught the force of this humanism if our pluralistic metaphor were mechanistic, so that all we could say about the city would be in terms of its physical characteristics. In thus continuing to grant a privileged status to the language of personhood, Christian theology will always leave its mark on any metaphysical framework in which it operates. This is true of Bonhoeffer's thought as it is of Karl Barth's.

The second qualification of this particular humanism is that its controlling image of man is of one who spoke in a particular way of a quite particular God. In the Jewish imagination of Jesus and in the Hebrew imagination of of his forebears, God was a quite personal figure with a definite character. Those who speak of the spirit of the city and whose imagination is informed by the biblical story will find that they are concerned with the realization of love and justice of the sort that concerned the men of that story, since it was the love and justice which they saw in their God. Imagining God as they did, they lived and spoke as they did and became the men they are presented to have been in that story. The character of that God, who loved righteousness like an Amos, agonized over the folly of his people like a Jeremiah, and loved like a Hosea, becomes central in the image of man for those informed by that story.

The conclusion of our investigation may be summarized as follows. The last writings of Bonhoeffer depict a certain form of human life. This is done in human terms, but mixed with it is some of the very oldest language of Christian theology. That some of this oldest language was no longer doing its old work, was acquiring a new meaning, is only another way of saying that it was being used in a new context and in a new way. Who can say how Bonhoeffer would have developed in his thinking and language had he lived? I make no pretense of holding him responsible for the analysis which I have made. In his last surviving writings, he was still exploring new uses of old words and therefore mixing these with some old uses. Understandably the results are often paradoxical. This analysis of one central paradox suggests that at least one way in which to move ahead from where Bonhoeffer was will lead us into a pluralistic metaphysics informed by a christological humanism, a view of the universe, a way of saying how things are in our pluralistic city, in which some men may live lives informed by the biblical story of a man who lived for others.

That is the hypothesis at which we arrive. Is it a good hypothesis? Is it useful? Is it true? Well, William James, I think, was right. The answer to that can only be found out by the man who dares to gamble on it. Bonhoeffer so gambled, and I gather he died convinced that he had won.

FAITH AND WORLDLINESS
IN BONHOEFFER'S THOUGHT

by Paul L. Lehmann

The response to Dietrich Bonhoeffer's fertile and
fragmentary theological ideas has been, in the main,
twofold. On the continent on which he lived and wrote,
suffered and died, he has been alternately hailed and
ignored. The response has been shaped by the Oder-
Neisse line. On the eastern side of that boundary, Bonhoeffer has been accepted, and even celebrated, as "the
prophet of a new Christianity," a phrase once used by
Professor Pauck to put a question to American theology
about Karl Barth.[1] To Christians living in a Marxist society the insights, style, and images which erupt from
the Bonhoeffer fragments nourish both the conversation
of the church with itself, in its preaching and teaching,
and the dialogue with Marxist unbelief and secularism.
The most perceptive interpretation of Bonhoeffer's
thought to date makes of him all but a Marxist, or at
least, the great Christian apostle to the Marxists.[2] As
Paul of Tarsus once went westward to the Gentiles, so
Bonhoeffer has reversed the direction and gone eastward
to the Gentiles of a world come of age.

[1] Wilhelm Pauck, *Karl Barth, Prophet of a New Christianity?*
(New York: Harper & Bros., 1931).
[2] Hanfried Mueller, *Von der Kirche zur Welt* (Leipzig: Koehler &
Amelang, 1961).

On the western side of the Oder-Neisse line, Bonhoeffer's thought has been both seriously probed and widely ignored. He has continued to speak to an inner company of his former students and companions in the struggle of the church against Hitler. This company has been joined by a larger circle in a series of annual conferences devoted to the clarification of Bonhoeffer's ideas and the assessment of their implications. This group has been responsible for an intermittently published periodical which bears the title of this volume, at least half of it. *Die Mündige Welt* (The World Come of Age) has appeared in four volumes between 1955 and 1963.[3] For the most part, however, it must be noted that Bonhoeffer has not seriously shifted the focus of attention of German theology from its concerns, on the one hand, with hermeneutics from Bultmann to Herbert Braun and, on the other hand, with neo-confessionalism in which the mentalities of the Barmen declaration and of Lutheran creedalism continue a debate on which fewer and fewer people listen in.

Meanwhile, in the United States the response to Bonhoeffer exhibits both enthusiasm and distortion. The enthusiasm is widespread among college students and the segment among them which finds its way into theological seminaries. The reasons for the enthusiasm are varied, and they do not mainly relate to his martyrdom. They relate rather to the candor and contemporaneity with which the language, ideas, and concerns of Bonhoeffer

[3] *Die Mündige Welt* (München: Chr. Kaiser, I, 1955; II, 1956; III, 1960; IV, 1963). Certain of the essays from these volumes have been published in English; *World Come of Age,* ed. R. Gregor Smith (Philadelphia: Fortress Press, 1967).

give life to the theological tradition and point to radical
new formulations which risk abandonment of tradition
rather than subject the reality and power of faith to its
deadening weight. Bonhoeffer seems to be concretely
involved in the critical struggle of faith with doubt
which characterizes serious theological curiosity today.
The curiosity may be coming alive or coming of age.
The response to Bonhoeffer is at least one important
measure of its sensitivity. Insofar as theological faculties
have lagged behind their students in this response, they
seem precariously prey to the dilemma between obso-
lescence and an *odium theologicum.*

The Distortion of the World Come of Age

We are more concerned, however, with the distortion
which afflicts the response to Bonhoeffer in this country.
It is not strange that the distortion should have focused
upon the phrase "the world come of age," since even
Bonhoeffer's closest students and friends have been puz-
zled by it and are still pursuing its implications. What *is*
strange is the expropriation of the phrase for purposes
alien to the intimate connection between Bonhoeffer's
own faith and spirit as a Christian and his theological
concerns. The phrase has, accordingly, functioned as a
misleading half-truth, carelessly and sometimes capri-
ciously disseminated. As such a half-truth, "the world
come of age" has supported the sloganizing of "the
death of God," of "holy worldliness," of "religionless
Christianity." Consequently, Bonhoeffer has been carica-
tured as the apostle of Christian atheism, the troubadour
of the new optimism, the St. George of the post-Christian

era whose sword of the secular spirit has decapitated the two-headed dragon (at least two) of tradition and transcendence. As Sigmund Freud once calmly addressed an imaginary believer, so Bonhoeffer is to be understood as having crusadingly addressed the Christianity which he was passing up and passing beyond. "I think," said Freud, "you are defending a lost cause. . . . My illusions are not, like religious ones, incapable of correction."[4]

Perhaps the most extreme form of this distortion has found its way into *The New York Review of Books*.[5] There Mr. William Bartley III, whose own odyssey has carried him beyond God to enlightenment, writes about Bonhoeffer as follows:

> It becomes rather urgent for a person holding a view like Bonhoeffer's—that there is literally no need for Christianity or for God in an adult world—to explain what if anything does distinguish a Christian from others, and why, indeed, anyone should in such circumstances remain a Christian. It is precisely at this point that Bonhoeffer, who is rarely profound but usually clear, becomes as vague as any conventional German theologian. The role of the Christian is conceived now as a fundamentally ethical one of total engagement in social and personal life in full collaboration with like-minded liberal secularists.

Mr. Bartley wonders also whether Bonhoeffer, had he not been executed, might not later have quite simply "forsaken Protestant theology."[6]

---

[4] Sigmund Freud, *The Future of an Illusion* (New York, 1964), pp. 87, 86. See also, Michael Novak, "Christianity: Renewed or Slowly Abandoned?" *Daedalus*, XCVI (Winter, 1967).

[5] W. W. Bartley III, "The Bonhoeffer Revival," *The New York Review of Books*, II (August 26, 1965). Quoted by Michael Novak in *op. cit.*, p. 239.

[6] Novak, *Ibid.*

Paul Tillich and Reinhold Niebuhr are even more condescendingly assessed. They are charged by Mr. Bartley with "shallow and wooly eclectic thinking" and with "occasional downright incompetence and self-deception." One might wonder how, in face of Bonhoeffer's conventional, German, theological vagueness Mr. Bartley can conclude so firmly that "the role of the Christian is conceived now as a fundamentally ethical one of total engagement in social and personal life in full collaboration with like-minded liberal secularists." More serious is the fallacy which enables Mr. Bartley to insist that, since for Bonhoeffer "there is literally no need for Christianity or for God in an adult world," he is required "to explain what if anything does distinguish a Christian from others, and why, indeed, anyone should in such circumstances remain a Christian." Only a little less ignorance of Bonhoeffer would tell an honest reader that this is exactly Bonhoeffer's point. The difference which being a Christian makes is not the need for Christianity or for God at all—in an adult world or some other world. According to Bonhoeffer, this has always been a grievous error of Christian preaching and teaching. The difference which being a Christian makes is simply faithfulness to the life of God in the world as this life takes shape in Jesus Christ and in human life. But then, as Michael Novak has remarked, Mr. Bartley has "registered a characteristic Anglo-American philosophical complaint."[7] To this complaint, Alasdair MacIntyre has replied with a not altogether dissimilar impertinence: "The

[7] *Ibid.*, p. 239.

creed of the English is that there is no God and that it is wise to pray to him from time to time."[8]

If Mr. Bartley's expropriation of the phrase "the world come of age" is a capricious dissemination of a half-truth, the expropriation of the phrase by the so-called "radical theologians" is, at the least, a careless dissemination of a half-truth. The carelessness is at once difficult to deal with and difficult to ignore because of the subtlety with which it makes "confusion worse confounded." Perhaps Professor William Hamilton is the most deliberate and strident disseminator of this subtle carelessness. His various attempts at it have been gathered together in a readily accessible paperback called, *Radical Theology and the Death of God*.[9] Professor Hamilton's acknowledged indebtedness to Bonhoeffer is candid and explicit.[10] At the same time, he recognizes that Bonhoeffer may not always be correctly understood as going as far as he is himself willing to go in the world come of age (DG, 39). The carelessness and the confusion, however, arise in this way. On the one hand, Hamilton writes: "We really don't know what Bonhoeffer meant by religion, and our modern study of the problem of religionlessness must be carried on quite independent of the task, probably fruit-

[8] Alasdair MacIntyre, "God and the Theologians," *Encounter*, XXI, No. 3; reprinted in part in David L. Edwards (ed.), *The Honest To God Debate* (Philadelphia: Westminster, 1963), pp. 215–28.

[9] Thomas J. Altizer and William Hamilton, *Radical Theology and the Death of God* (New York: Bobbs-Merrill Co., 1966).

[10] Hamilton's essays, in the paperback just noted, which underlie this interpretation are: *The Death of God Theologies Today*, (1963; DG); *Thursday's Child* (1964; TC); *Dietrich Bonhoeffer* (1965; DB); *The New Optimism* (1966; NO). The references will be abbreviated in the text as indicated by the letter symbols.

less, of establishing just what Bonhoeffer meant" (DG, 39). On the other hand, he writes: "Technically, what Bonhoeffer is saying is that in the modern world that can do without God, the idea of the innate religiousness of man, the religious *a priori* must be rejected. . . . Put more clearly, Bonhoeffer states that in the world come of age, we can no longer be religious, if religion is defined as that system that treats God or the gods as need-fulfillers and problem-solvers" (DB, 117, 116). If we really don't know what Bonhoeffer meant by religion, how can we say "technically, what Bonhoeffer is saying?" Nor is it easy to understand why Professor Hamilton would state clearly what Bonhoeffer says about religion in an essay admittedly written for "an audience that had no special background information about the current theological influence exercised by Bonhoeffer" (DB, 112), having said already two years earlier, in a self-styled "programmatic essay" (DG, 22) that we probably could never establish what Bonhoeffer meant.

Fortunately for this volume Dr. Eberhard Bethge, holder in 1966–67 of the Fosdick Professorship in Union Seminary, has happily agreed to address himself to the very question Dr. Hamilton says we don't really know anything about. Thus, the record is in imminent prospect of being set straight, supported, beyond Dr. Bethge's essay to come, by the recent publication of Dr. Bethge's long-awaited, full-length biography, with which Bonhoeffer himself at last has a chance of coming of age in a world come of age.[11] "Those who do not believe in

[11] Eberhard Bethge, *Dietrich Bonhoeffer* (München: Chr. Kaiser Verlag, 1967). The English translation is already in preparation.

God," the President Emeritus of Princeton Seminary was wont to remark, "are not prepared to take account of undesigned coincidence." At least by charter, Union Seminary still does. To the Seminary's own archival recollections of one of its notable alumni may thus be added, both as a *coincidentia oppositorum* and as a *coincidentia providentiae,* the notation that Dr. Bethge's impressive biographical achievement and his incumbency in the Fosdick Chair happened together. (This is a happening that even Thomas Hoving missed.)

Meanwhile, we shall venture to risk the opinion that Dr. Hamilton's distortion of the phrase "the world come of age" will be, like Freud's illusions, capable of correction by the record. Hamilton's careless subtlety will then stand exposed by the careful subtlety of Bonhoeffer himself. The critical instance of the exposure takes us to the center of our present task.

The relation between faith and worldliness in Bonhoeffer's thought is a dialectical one. Like the relation between God and the world come of age, between Christology and religionless Christianity, between church and humanity, theology and ethics, forgiveness and love, hiddenness and openness in the life of discipleship—or any other combination among the characteristic Bonhoeffer themes—and not least, Bonhoeffer himself in a world come of age—there is a single focus of a many-faceted preoccupation which functions as the clue to a correct assessment of Bonhoeffer's thought and of his contribution to the theological unrest and adventure of the present time. I owe to Dr. Bethge the proper language for Bonhoeffer's consuming theological concern and for his dialectical analysis and application of it. The concern is with Jesus Christ: with who Jesus Christ is for us today and with what it means today to be a Christian. Today is the world come of age. The relation of Jesus Christ to this "today," to the world come of age, is the dialectical one of "identity and identification" (Bethge). How can a Christian discover and respond to his identity as a Christian without weakening or surrendering his identification with the world? How can a Christian identify with the world without losing or abandoning his identity as a Christian?

Professor Hamilton clearly and correctly sees the central importance of these questions to Bonhoeffer's thought. He wrestles with them himself with such earnestness, fascination, and candor as to confess that, as a theologian, he does not know whether "we discovered this (i.e., his own role as a theologian) in him, and then in ourselves, or in ourselves, and then rejoiced to find it in him" (TC, 93). He struggles to maintain the depth, range, and persistence of Bonhoeffer's subtlety in probing the problem of identity and identification. "The Christian life," he declares,

> as the discernment of Jesus beneath the worldly masks can be called work or interpretation or criticism; while the Christian life as becoming Jesus looks a little different. At this point the Christian is the sucker, the fall guy, the jester, the fool for Christ, the one who stands before Pilate and is silent, the one who stands before power and power-structures and laughs. Whichever of the paths one takes to find or define Jesus in the world . . . the worldliness of the Protestant can never . . . have an utterly humanistic form. I may be proposing . . . a too narrowly ethical approach to Christo-

> logical problems, but it should at least be noted that however acute the experience of the death of God may be for us . . . a form of obedience remains to us in our time of deprivation (DG, 50).

But then he seems to waver after all in the dialectical subtlety of his concern to keep identity and identification together. "We are the not-havers, whose undialectical *yes* to the world is balanced by a *no* to God," he declares in his enthusiastic optimism (NO, 169). "The combination of a certain kind of God-rejection with a certain kind of world-affirmation is the point where I join the death of God movement," he goes on.

> This faith is more like a place, a being with or standing beside the neighbor. Faith has almost collapsed into love, and the Protestant is no longer defined as the forgiven sinner, . . . but as the one beside the neighbor, beside the enemy, at the disposal of man in need. . . . Really to travel along this road means that we trust the world, not God, to be our fulfiller and problem solver, and God, if he is to be for us at all, must come in some other role (DG, 36, 37, 40).

But for Professor Hamilton God does not come; at least, not yet. There is only undialectical waiting, only the possibility of a presence, only the place beside the neighbor, as the place "where Jesus is to be found and served" (DG, 50).

Professor Hamilton's treatment of Bonhoeffer, and of his own relation to him, is significant for the present attempt to explore the relation between faith and worldliness in Bonhoeffer's thought because it shows not only what can happen to Bonhoeffer in a world come of age, but also what can happen to a world come of age when

Bonhoeffer's subtle probing of the dialectic between identity and identification is abandoned. Faith does indeed collapse into love; and love collapses into the neighbor; and the neighbor into Christ; and Christ into man; and man into the optimistic worldliness by which, in a marked inversion of Mr. Auden, not of tragedy but of anxiety, man knows how to place every "what" in his world, including why he is both God and good.[12] We do not wish to extol Bonhoeffer either as the architect or the patron theologian of a world come of age. We do raise the question, however, whether it is theologically admissible to play games with Bonhoeffer's language and ideas; and more especially, of whether a closer attention to Bonhoeffer's own dialectic might point to more creative relations between faith and worldliness than that proposed by a self-styled radical theology, namely, the death of God in a world come of age. This is not an occasion for gamesmanship, even if there were time. It is, however, a time and an occasion to note some aspects of Bonhoeffer's analysis of the dialectical relation between faith and worldliness with particular reference to their bearing upon the difficult task of being a Christian today without losing either one's identity or one's identification.

The Dialectic Between Faith and Worldliness

The dialectic between faith and worldliness is the ethical mode of the basic and inescapable dialectic of a Christian between identity and identification. The relation between faith and worldliness characterizes the behavior of a Christian in the world. As Bonhoeffer sees it,

[12] W. H. Auden, *The Age of Anxiety* (New York: Random House, 1947), p. 24.

there is no true worldliness without faith; and contrariwise, there is no true faith without worldliness. Ultimately, for Bonhoeffer, there is only one proper adjective for worldliness. It is the adjective "Christian." For semantic and cultural reasons, however, it is impossible to speak of "Christian worldliness." The christological reading of reality which underlies this phrase is a biblical option which can only function as an option in a pluralistic world of rival idolatries and competing ideologies. Freud, and his disciples and correctors, are but the latest documentors of the fact that the "reality-principle" has always had hard going in a world in which illusions are hard to break and fulfilling loyalties hard to come by. On the reality question the church has done no better than the world; the world is now trying once again to do better than the church. Bonhoeffer's own odyssey, which Dr. Bethge has described and documented with brilliant care, as a movement from theologian to Christian and from Christian to contemporary, is his own best commentary upon his relentless responsiveness to this reality, however radically its language and structures in church and world might have to be revised. Thus, he declares in his *Ethics,*

> There are not two realities but only one reality. This is the reality of God in the reality of the world, revealed in Christ. Participating in Christ, we stand at one and the same time, in the reality of God and in the reality of the world. The reality of Christ includes within itself the reality of the world. . . . It is a denial of the revelation of God in Jesus Christ to wish to be "Christian," without seeing and recognizing the world in Christ.[13]

[13] *Ethik* (München: Chr. Kaiser, 1949), p. 62. Translation mine.

The risk of faulty seeing is so great that Bonhoeffer will not speak of "Christian worldliness" but rather of "true worldliness" (*echte Weltlichkeit*).

In a world come of age, it is particularly important to bear this in mind. Otherwise, we shall needlessly have to live down the radical theology. The christological leverage for Bonhoeffer's view of reality I shall leave to Dr. Bethge's subsequent discussion. Meanwhile, let us content ourselves with his reminder that

> Bonhoeffer often expressed the view that the *Ethics* was to be his life's task. . . . The concept of "reality," already intimated in *Act and Being*, . . . is developed (in the *Ethics*) in new ways and appears as tightly anchored in Christology. . . . In this way Bonhoeffer tries to avoid both the positivistic and the idealistic understanding of reality. He regarded both as abstractions. . . . He wished (also) to circumnavigate the reefs and rocks (*Klippen*) of a merely actualistic situation-ethic, and yet retain its proper concern. He wished also to overcome the pale remoteness of a normative ethic, and yet take up its concern about continuity. Thus, again, he wished to mediate between two contradictory positions.[14]

In *The Cost of Discipleship*, Bonhoeffer was almost monastically scornful of the world. In the light of his concentration there upon the glorification of Christ, the world appears under the heavy shadow of negation. A kind of ultra-Lutheranism seems to lurk beneath the surface of his description of discipleship and threatens to exchange an Augustinian Luther for a Franciscan one. As Dr. Bethge's biography now helps us to see more clearly, however, what was really going on, on the way

[14] Bethge, *op. cit.,* pp. 804–5. Parentheses and translation mine.

from *The Cost of Discipleship* to the *Ethics,* that is, from 1937 to 1945, was a steady and dynamic preoccupation with the dialectic between faith and worldliness.[15] The movement was a shift of attention from the response to the Lordship of Christ in the church to the response to the Lordship of Christ in and over the world. The terms of the shift concerned the relation between the command of God, as *primus usus legis,* and the mandates under which and through which the Christian lives in the world; more strongly even, through which the world is structured or conformed to the world-reality of Christ. As Bethge has put it: "The church had claimed Bonhoeffer's attention for such a long time that the world in its creatureliness and historicality (*Geschöpflichkeit und Geschichtlichkeit*) had—with good reason—gone unnoticed. Now, the world claimed fresh attention as the sphere of the *regnum Christi.*"[16] The mandates carry the formative behavioral load of this thrust towards worldliness. The first use of the term "mandates" was explicitly used in relation to the conception of the *regnum Christi* and especially as a substitute for the dangerous notion of the "orders of creation" which had characterized Protestant theology and ethics since the Reformation. Even the notion of "orders of providence," which had appeared in the first try at the *Ethics,* was abandoned in favor of mandates. The mandates function for Bonhoeffer as the guidelines of "true worldliness." They do this partly because they express the relation of man to the world as the sphere of Christ's rule; partly because they indicate

[15] *Ibid.,* pp. 805 ff.
[16] *Ibid.,* pp. 805–6. Translation mine.

the concreteness of the claim of Christ in every identification with and task in the world; and partly because in this way whoever takes responsibility in the world for the world is given freedom of action and real history takes place (Bethge).

The list and explanation of the mandates raise the question whether the English translation, "divine decree" for *göttliches Mandat,* says exactly what Bonhoeffer wished to express. For Bonhoeffer, "mandate" refers to a human structure in the world which functions in a basic way to express and to order God's purpose for the world. God's purpose is that the world shall be the place of the humanization of man, as Jesus Christ gives form and freedom and fulfillment to all that man is and does, is intended to become and can become. Bonhoeffer arrives at these structures through a reading of the Bible in the context of human history, sociology, and politics. He finds these structures confirmed through a reading of human history, sociology, and politics in the context of the Bible. Here too the dialectic of faith and worldliness is operative in his thought. In Bonhoeffer's own words, "we understand by 'mandate,' a concrete, divine task, grounded in the revelation in Christ and attested in the Scriptures. Furthermore, a 'mandate' is the power and authorization for carrying out a specific divine command, the bestowal (*Verleihung*) of divine authority upon an earthly situation."[17] The mandates are four in number. They are operational structures particularly appropriate to the doing in a world come of age of the will of God. Bonhoeffer's word is *Gestalten.* The structures or *Gestalten*

---

[17] Bonhoeffer, *Ethik,* p. 222. Translation mine.

of "Christian worldliness," therefore, are: church, marriage and family, culture, and authority (*Obrigkeit*).

Our purpose here is not to follow through on Bonhoeffer's account of these mandates in operation. We are concerned with emphasizing that they provide the structures of true worldliness through which the dialectic between faith and worldliness shows itself in behavior. Two letters to Bethge must suffice in support of our suggestion that faith and worldliness belong together; and that when seen in their interchangeability, Bonhoeffer's contribution to a world come of age is his restless and openended search for ever new language and ever more concrete ways of keeping the identity of a Christian in the world and the identification of a Christian with the world together.

On June 25, 1942, he wrote:

My strong activity along the worldly sector in recent days ever and again gives me pause. I am astonished at myself that I live and can live for days without reading the Bible. (Were I to force myself to it, I should find that autosuggestion.) I understand that such autosuggestion can be a great help and is; but I am afraid that along this route, a genuine experience could be falsified and not lead to genuine help after all. When, then, I turn to the Bible again, the book becomes new for me and a joy as never before, and I have the urge once again to preach. . . . I sense how the opposition to everything "religious" grows in me. . . . But of God and of Christ, I must continually think. My great concern is with integrity, freedom, compassion. . . . In this sense, I understand my present doings on the worldly sector.[18]

[18] Bethge, *op. cit.*, pp. 810–11. Translation mine.

Two years later, on January 23, 1944, he wrote with special reference to friendship:

> It is not easy to give a sociological account of friendship. Friendship probably belongs under the conceptions of culture . . . and education. . . . Marriage, work, state, and church have their concrete divine command. But what about culture and education? . . . They do not belong to the sphere of obedience but to the sphere of freedom which surrounds all three mandates. He who does not know about this sphere [*Spielraum*] of freedom, can be a good father, citizen, and worker, and even a good Christian. But I question whether he can be a complete human being (and to this extent cannot really be a Christian in the full sense). Perhaps—so it almost seems today—it is the conception of the church which alone offers an understanding of the sphere of freedom (art, learning, friendship, play)? Thus, the "aesthetic existence" (Kierkegaard) would be not alien to the church but really to be newly established within it. Who, for example, can nourish without difficulty in our time, music or friendship or play or joy? Certainly not the "ethical man" but only the Christian. . . . I think that within the realm of freedom, understood in this way, . . . friendship is the rarest and most expensive good. . . .[19]

This is the subtle dialectic of faith and worldliness which arrests the so-called radical theology's distortion of the world come of age and makes Bonhoeffer a more profound resource of celebration of and in the secular city.

The Secret Discipline of Faith

There is, however, an aspect of the dialectic between faith and worldliness which calls for some attention before we suspend the present consideration. It has to do

[19] Bonhoeffer, *Ethik*, pp. 222–23. Translation mine.

with one of the more obscure and problematical of Bonhoeffer's thoughts about the dialectic of identity and
identification. Perhaps also for this reason it has been insufficiently noticed. I refer to what I have ventured to
describe by the phrase "the secret discipline of faith."
Bonhoeffer's own word for it is *Arkandisciplin*. In the
course of a long letter to Bethge, April 30, 1944, Bonhoeffer came to the question of the biblical message and
the modern man. "Are not righteousness and the king-
dom of God on earth the center of everything?" he asked.
"The real concern is not with the Beyond but with this
world, how it was created, how it will be sustained, held
in order, reconciled and renewed. What goes beyond the
world, and is according to the gospel, must be for the
world." And then, following his strictures against Karl
Barth's revelational positivism, he declares: "There must
be a restoration of an arcane discipline, through which
the mysteries of Christian faith may be preserved from
profanation."[20] What is this arcane discipline? And what
is its relation to "true worldliness" in a world come of
age?[21]

The phrase seems to refer to an earlier experience of
the church in a world come of age. This time the church
had come into the world. In our time, the world is leaving
the church behind. But in both instances, the dialectic
between identity and identification takes similar forms.

[20] Dietrich Bonhoeffer, *Widerstand und Ergebung* (München:
Chr. Kaiser, 1952), pp. 184–85.
[21] There is an instructive discussion of the whole problem by
Gisela Meuss in Vol. III of *Die Mündige Welt* (München: Chr.
Kaiser, 1960). Miss Meuss's essay is entitled *Arkandisziplin und
Weltlichkeit bei Dietrich Bonhoeffer* (pp. 68–115). The citations
below follow Miss Meuss.

In the post-Constantinian era, as Lietzmann has noted, "the church became an essential element of public life; she became an indispensable part of the world which she had hitherto passionately fought against" (72). As a defense both against the confusion of Christian mysteries with secular ones, as well as against the mere externalizing of Christianity in the world, the church laid great stress upon the painstaking ordering of its own life in worship and catechesis. When the post-Christian era began to dawn, well before anybody suspected what was going on, the church, this time also in the context of the Reformation, gave special concern to the distinction between the baptized and the unbaptized, between those prepared to receive the Eucharist and those excluded from it. The theologians of the seventeenth century called this practice of special stress upon worship and catechesis, "arcane discipline."

Bonhoeffer seems to have returned to this tradition. "What is the meaning of worship and prayer," he asks, "in a religionless time? Does an arcane discipline acquire now . . . new significance?" (71). And so, in our turn, we might ask, how Bonhoeffer could put these questions without drawing back from a world come of age and into a revival of the Constantinian spirit, of a *corpus Christi* within a *corpus christianium?* Does the secret discipline of faith not cut the gordian knot of the dialectic between faith and worldliness so necessary to keep identity and identification together?

That Bonhoeffer did explore and even propose such an arcane discipline can scarcely be denied. Already in the *Sanctorum communio,* he lays great stress upon the visible church, upon the word and sacrament, upon Bible study and prayer as marks of the sociological reality of the church as a community of faith in relation to the communities of the world. In *The Cost of Discipleship*, he seems to stress even more strongly the separation of the Christian from the world and the hiddenness of the devout life. And even in the *Ethics*, the mandate of the church penetrates all the other mandates, even as it penetrates the whole of mankind.

Inconclusive as they must remain, there are perhaps two things to be said in conclusion about the secret discipline of faith. The first is, that unlike its previous uses, the arcane discipline is radically instrumental to the *regnum Christi* in the world. This means that for Bonhoeffer, the discipline of faith is necessary to keep identification of the Christian with the world from swallowing up his identity. If one recalls Professor Hamilton's readiness to wait for a possible arrival of a God whose presence can now at best be expected, Bonhoeffer's waiting is neither empty of activity, nor completely filled with neighbor identification. He knows something about the relation of prayer and fasting to the casting out of demons. The second remark pertinent to the secret discipline of faith in Bonhoeffer's thought is that its traditional forms were pursued in a pragmatic and functional way. He did not find it necessary to say an undialectical "no" to God in order to say an undialectical "yes" to the world. Thus, he ventured to risk something concrete on behalf of the identity of the Christian in the hope that thereby his identification with the world might bring its true identity to the world itself. In his own life, it

44

worked. He died as a theologian and a Christian who had become a contemporary. If, in a world come of age, we wish to pursue the dialectic between faith and worldliness without surrendering our identity as Christians to identification with the world, and thus betraying the world, we must ask ourselves how we propose to nourish identity so that identification may be protected against idolatry and ideology and thus bless the world and all men therein with freedom, fulfillment, and joy.

BONHOEFFER'S CHRISTOLOGY AND HIS "RELIGIONLESS CHRISTIANITY"[1]

by EBERHARD BETHGE

In the theology of Dietrich Bonhoeffer there exists an intimate connection between Christology and a non-religious expression of the witness for Christ, although the specific formulation—non-religious interpretation—did not originate until near the end of his life. There was, to be sure, a kind of joyful surprise about his new point of departure in April, 1944, when Bonhoeffer formulated the new task. But even he sensed that its newness could not deny what was surely continuous in his life and thought. His mind had been occupied with the issue for many years. It can be shown today that the theme of "non-

[1] The phrase "religionless Christianity" has been included in the title of this essay because the English-speaking world discusses Bonhoeffer's later utterances under this formula. Throughout this essay, however, I prefer to use the phrase "non-religious interpretation," since the German discussion concentrates almost exclusively on this formula.

The difference is not merely one of terms or phrases. It reflects a difference in theological orientation and Bonhoeffer cannot help but be interpreted in terms of the orientation of each of his interpreters. This tendency, however,—for the English-speaking world to concentrate on matters of worship, institutions, and social action, and for the German-speaking world to focus on matters of exegesis and preaching—does not always do justice to the total Bonhoeffer, for it isolates and sometimes manipulates him to fit within the particular tradition of his interpreters.

Bonhoeffer himself used the term "religionless Christianity" only in the first theological letter from Tegel, April 30, 1944 (twice

religious interpretation" is present and working in the many different approaches he took in his writings, no matter how conservative or "religious" those writings may now appear.

The thesis of this essay, therefore, is that Bonhoeffer's "non-religious interpretation" is first and last "christological" interpretation; and, in reverse, that his Christology always tried to present itself in the form of non-religious interpretation. This interrelation was so vital for Bonhoeffer that he lost interest when the two elements were separated: *Christology* not qualified by something like non-religious interpretation became an unrelated entity and suffered a fatal loss of reality; *non-religious Christianity* without Christocentrism became a Sisyphean endeavor of modern man to adjust to a newly discovered self and world.

The Thoroughgoing Theme: Christology

For the first claim that non-religious interpretation means christological interpretation there is agreement

there), i.e., just when starting his new approach. The phrase used in all the following letters is "non-religious interpretation" or some closely connected derivative (about eleven times).

Bonhoeffer's term is in no sense limited only to exegesis and better preaching, for his attack on present institutional and creedal establishments of Christianity was no less than revolutionary. But in his task he preferred the more modest label of "interpretation." Interpretation begins with careful listening to the apostles and to the Fathers; never would Bonhoeffer claim that his theological position originated *de novo*.

Therefore, in August, 1944, when Bonhoeffer began the manuscript for his book which was lost in prison, he said both that "the Church must come out of its stagnation" and that "it is only in the spirit of prayer that any such work can be begun and carried through" (LP 208). Or as he put it in an even more urgent double question, "How do we speak . . . in a 'secular' way about 'God'? In what way are we 'religionless-secular' Christians . . . ?" (LP 153).

among the few serious experts on Bonhoeffer. John Godsey was the first to inform the English-speaking world about the foundation of Bonhoeffer's late utterances in his earlier Christocentric books. Gerhard Ebeling and Ronald Gregor Smith have drawn Bonhoeffer's christological efforts into Bultmannian and Gogartian channels. Hanfried Mueller, the Marxist theologian, has translated "religionless Christianity" directly into "churchless Christianity," but in contrast to the optimistic theologians of the secular at work in America, he has developed his anti-ecclesiasticism out of a deep-rooted Lutheran and Barthian *theologia crucis.* More recently, J. A. Phillips has found two contradictory Christologies in Bonhoeffer.[2] And Heinrich Ott has recently uncovered elements of neothomistic and de Chardinian Christo-universalism.[3]

There is indeed no difficulty in demonstrating explicitly Bonhoeffer's essential Christocentrism which, to be sure, remained trinitarian, as the main trend in his writings. In 1927, in *Sanctorum Communio,* the quest for Christ's presence is developed under the formula "Christ existing as church" (*Christus als Gemeinde existierend*)—the church as a community of persons. In 1935, we find the same quest for Christ's presence in Bonhoeffer's emphasis on actual, visible discipleship, without any eschatological reservations—this against the early Barth; on the other hand against Emanuel Hirsch, Paul Althaus, and Emil Brunner, he does not give way to the natural the-

[2] *Christ for Us in the Theology of Dietrich Bonhoeffer* (New York: Harper & Row, 1967).

[3] *Wirklichkeit und Glaube, I—zum theologischen Erbe Dietrich Bonhoeffers* (Zurich: Vandenhoeck & Ruprecht, 1966).

ologies; and against the German-Aryan heresy he deliberately repeats Christ's title as "Son of David," and for the same reason he even embarks upon an "unscientific" christological exegesis of the Old Testament. In 1942 we find, against a static Lutheran separation of the two realms, the quest for Christ's presence in ethical responsibility for the concrete, guilt-covered world. Finally, in 1944, the presence of Christ is found in the conformation of man with Christ's messianic suffering, risking a "church" which allows itself to be drawn anonymously into the world. This is the seldom recognized but ever present combination of Bonhoeffer's non-religious interpretation with the *Arcandiscipline*.

An Analysis of Bonhoeffer's Life-Question: "Who Is Christ for Us Today?"

In Bonhoeffer's 1933 lectures on Christology (*Christ the Center*) our theme assumes the distinct form of a constant question, "Who are You?" and this question shapes the peculiar architecture of the lectures. This same concern directs more than ever the meditations of Tegel from 1944, now put in an enlarged but less generalized way: "Who is Christ for us today?" And it is this enlargement, as we will see, that makes all the difference.

Contrary to some scholarly opinion, one can see that Bonhoeffer's concern in 1944 was not merely an hermeneutical device for interpreting old biblical documents, nor an outline for a program of "religionless Christianity," nor a phenomenological study of "man coming of age."

Such interpretations, programs, and analyses are only subparagraphs under the one over-arching question, which, four times repeated, puts the catch phrases in proper perspective. Bonhoeffer did not ask, "What selection of biblical treasures and ecclesiastical concepts can we still offer to the modern world?" This kind of question would turn Bonhoeffer into the reductionist he never wanted to be. Nor did he ask, "How may we better communicate to modern man the message we possess?" That question would turn the interpreter into a salesman to the have-nots. Barth did not come close to understanding Bonhoeffer when he drew a caricature of him in *The Humanity of God*:

> A little "non-religious" language from the street, the newspaper, literature, and, if one is ambitious, from the philosopher may thus, for the sake of communication, occasionally indeed be in order. However, we should not become particularly concerned about this. A little of the language of Canaan, a little "revelation-positivism," can also be a good thing . . . understood even by the oddest strangers.[4]

Already in 1932 Bonhoeffer had said, "The point is not how are we to model the message, but what really *is* the message and its content?"

Bonhoeffer became "evangelistic" only by asking this one central question, "Who are You for us today?" and by pointing to an answer with fragmentary probes and with his life. For Bonhoeffer this question was based on three presuppositions: a humble one, a critical one, and a hopeful one:

[4] (Richmond: John Knox Press, 1960), p. 59. Quoted by permission of the publisher.

First, the question is *humble* because it asks about Christ *for us today,* yet recognizes that He is the Christ who is already given. He is not the problem, we are. Bonhoeffer was not pessimistic, as Gogarten or Heim sometimes were, about this world as Christ's world. Out of an unshaken faith in the presence of Christ he neither asks nor answers the weak and pretentious question, "Does modern secular man need Christ?" Christ *is* there and we have to answer the challenge negatively or positively. This presupposition sets Bonhoeffer apart from those who still want to reestablish a place for religion in the world. He does not apologetically seek for a God in ultimate human concern or in the private spheres of a religious meaning of life. In Bonhoeffer's question there is the humility and the certainty of the man who knows whom he is going to meet.

But the question is, secondly, also *critical.* It acknowledges that the old christological answers may no longer carry the meaning they once expressed. Those answers, when their vocabulary was current coinage, lifted up, corrected, and put to shame. But repetition has emptied the words. Instead of mediating genuine liberation in the Christ-encounter they have become obstacles or barriers to the discovery of Him. Christological titles have turned into expensive passports into the realm of faith.

Thirdly, the question is, however, *hopeful.* Though deeply indebted to the language of the Fathers and impressed by the sudden discovery of their wisdom in the German church struggle, Bonhoeffer knew that the challenge of Christ's presence includes the risk and the promise of a new, relevant christological language. We will see later how he tried to meet this challenge.

It is the strict personalistic way of asking "*Who* is he?" that separates Bonhoeffer's work from the detached research on the place of religion in life, from the apologetic defenses of ultimate meaning or of still valuable provinces where "God-talk" is possible. He does not allow himself to be shifted into the question, "What is this man all about?"; rather, he constantly sticks to the question, "Who is he?" Unfortunately there are several mistranslations in *Letters and Papers from Prison;* it should say "Who," not "What." (This has been corrected in the new translation.) In his Christology lectures of 1933, Bonhoeffer made a strong point about the basic importance of the Who-question, resisting the objectifying, self-integrating How- and What-questions:

> The question "Who?" is the question of transcendence. . . . The question "Who?" expresses the strangeness and otherness of the encounter and at the same time reveals itself as the question of the very existence of the enquirer himself. . . . It is the question about love for one's neighbour. The questions of transcendence and existence become a personal question. That means that man cannot answer the question "Who?" by himself. . . . The question "Who?" presupposes an answer that has already been given. . . .

And again,

> The question is reversed. . . . "Who are you, to ask thus?" . . . "Who are you, who can still only inquire after me when I restore you, justify you and give you my grace?" The christological question "Who?" is finally formulated only where this reversed question is also heard (CC 30–34).

This matter was in Bonhoeffer's mind in the letters when he asked again, "Who is he?" and when he asked for a new encounter in which one is to risk his own structures and be drawn into His being. In the *Ethics* he called this being conformed to Christ's *Gestalt;* and in the letters being drawn into his messianic suffering. He considers this to be more of a question of faith, as distinct from questions of "religion."

While still grounded in the principles of 1933, Bonhoeffer's question assumed a new form in 1944: "Who is He 'for us today?'" This indicates that the 1933 Bonhoeffer might be characterized by a lack of questioning (*Frageversäumnis*) and a lack of reality-relatedness (*Wirklichkeitsbezug*); Heinrich Ott recently accused Barth of that very thing. But now in 1944, Bonhoeffer says, *"for us today."*

Of whom is Bonhoeffer speaking when he refers to the contemporary "us"? Bonhoeffer literally thinks of himself and his ecclesiastical friends and the non-ecclesiastically minded co-conspirators in his family who were willing to serve a coming society. "Us" refers to men who are related to each other in sharing guilt for the past and in common destinies for the future. Yet on a deeper level the "us" includes men who understand themselves as (a) heirs of a specific Christian religious tradition; (b) members of a society in the process of coming of age; and (c) as such, men called to faith in the presence of Christ.

It is necessary that we understand Bonhoeffer's specific usage of the term "religion." He had ceased to differentiate between false and true religion; rather, he drew a distinction, learned from Luther, between faith and religion—religion coming from the flesh, but faith from the Spirit. Like some European contemporaries, Bonhoeffer could call men's ultimate desires for meaning and confirmation "religion." Yet the adjective "religious" had since 1927 become for him a purely critical label, as is evidenced by his use of the term throughout his writing from *Act and Being* to the *Letters*. A quarrel about the suitability of this terminology, however, may lead us away from the points he did make, for we have not been able to replace satisfactorily the controversial label until now.

Bonhoeffer's "religious Christianity" can be summarized in line with some of his explicit definitions and some implicit conclusions drawn from his thoughts in *Letters and Papers from Prison:* Bonhoeffer calls the *metaphysical* dressing of biblical faith "religion." Metaphysics here means a conceptualization of the message within the philosophical framework of both the Greeks and the idealistic philosophers of the nineteenth century. Once bold and conquering attempts to express the relevance of the gospel, those conceptualizations have become preconditions for faith. Their character of additive superstructure, providing meaning and ultimacy for life, made them guarantors and protectors of existing orders and establishments, pacifying the disturbing revolutionary elements of the Jesus of the Sermon on the Mount. Christianity had come to mean thinking in terms of two static realms, while it emphasized its own character as a religion of deliverance from this world. Religion as an additional factor of life had become a partial province of the whole, which resulted philosophically in the subtle doctrine of a religious *a priori* in man. Bonhoeffer calls metaphysical religion "a partial extension of the world" (LP 209), which has lost its threatening and uplifting transcendence. He wished, however, to relocate genuine transcendence in this world—in the person next to me.

Bonhoeffer describes the *individualistic* handling of the message as "religion." The Lutheran emphasis on soteriology had resulted in a "My-Lord-and-me and me-and-my-Lord" piety. The final privacy of faith led to an elimination or sterilization of basic elements in the Bible. Many find this individualistic privacy still at work in Bultmann's existential interpretation of *Selbstverständnis;* therefore Bonhoeffer can say that "Bultmann did not go far enough." Again, "religious Christianity" is made a partial province of life, its domain cut out from the relevant spheres of life by the secularization of even the last unenlightened provinces of individual life. Against this, Bonhoeffer wrote, "the 'religious act' is always something partial; 'faith' is something whole, involving the whole of one's life" (LP 199). In this process of provincialization all attention is focused on the boundaries of the realm of religion; they must be properly watched and preserved, and they foster a spirit of defensiveness as a result of which there is "no taking risks for others" (LP 209).

For Bonhoeffer the religious concept of the *Deus ex machina* stands over against the biblical breakthrough of a suffering Christ. Christian religion had become the problem-solver, the answerer of last questions, the escape into surrogate fulfillments. Religion exists by the power of God, but Bonhoeffer wrote, "The Bible directs [the Christian] to God's powerlessness and suffering" (LP 197).

Religion has shaped Christianity in such a way that it developed the *privileged* class of the initiated over the outsiders—"heathens," unbelievers, atheists—making that privileged class in the eyes of the latter the dominant imperialists. Religious activities had become the luxury of certain classes who could afford or who had to afford the time. One first *has* to be a part of this class to maintain his bourgeois respectability and then one *wants* to belong to it in order to retain the existing orders of power and ways of thought. The Christian religion had set up guardianship relations to men, held under tutelage of priests as the mediators of life and of pastors and theologians as the administrators of truth. The patronizing, feudalistic character of Christian institutions and creeds had transformed the freeing majesty of the powerless servanthood of Christ into power-structures of sterilizing dependencies. Bonhoeffer, therefore, can speak of violation, "religious compulsion" (LP 153).

This is for Bonhoeffer the actual religious tradition which has shaped the institutions and concepts of the Christian Western world and which has provoked a wealth of polemical reaction, and he considers himself a solidaristic but critical member of that world.

Turning to Bonhoeffer's concept of a world coming of age, we see that the phrase is a description of a given process within Western civilization, not a statistical calculation on a man-made chart of human progress. Note that he usually says "world which is becoming of age" or "has come of age," and very seldom, "world come of age." In his earlier years he was able to use the term which for a long time had shaped the churches' attitude to its surrounding world, viz., *secularization*. In this term the churches had taken a condescending attitude toward a whole period of history. Yet after 1939 Bonhoeffer never used this term again, recognizing its deploring and degrading character. During the first month of his theological writing in Tegel (April, May, and beginning of June, 1944) he spoke of the "autonomy" of the Western trends in science, politics, the arts, and philosophy. Only in June did the term "coming of age" suddenly appear and then Bonhoeffer held onto it with noticeable joy. He used the term in allusion to what he had learned from Kant who described the Enlightenment as the "exodus of man, responsible himself, from his not having come of age. . . . Not being of age is the inability of man to use his own reason without the guidance of others."[5]

Bonhoeffer's idea is that the present period of our history "without God" should be blessed rather than condemned. The genesis of this concept is his Christology; the cross of Christ not only judges and delivers the world, but also gives it freedom to be what it is in its own worldly structures. The notion "coming of age" is for Bonhoeffer, therefore, not the sum total of all those men who have reached maturity but a living declaration, a necessary risk in granting what in an unreversible process of adolescence each man and group deserves.

[5] Immanuel Kant, Werke, I (1960), p. 163.

This means that Bonhoeffer never pointed to an optimistic analysis of man as becoming better and better, "happy in his secularity and free of guilt," as Fackenheim makes Bonhoeffer say.[6] The main notion for Bonhoeffer is "responsibility," the unreversible capability and duty of adults individually to answer the questions of life in their own particular fields and within their own autonomous structures. This includes, to be sure, the joy which follows when human beings grow into their own manhood, but it also includes the integration of historical determinations, guilt, failures, and visions as well. Nobody makes adults children again; they stay responsible even when they turn childish, immature, or tyrannical.

Bonhoeffer wished that the contemporary church would bless those periods of earthly history which she had for the last centuries only judged, leading to fatal results for both. Similarly, she should now judge where she had blessed too long and too readily. Bonhoeffer believed that the declaration "coming of age," in close connection with and out of his faith in the presence of the Crucified One, prevents the blessing from becoming a cheap adjustment to modern man. Christology protects man come of age from deifying or demonizing his secularity again, and from falling into hopeless skepticism.

To whom is Bonhoeffer referring when, in the early Forties, he speaks of "man come of age"? He speaks to

[6] "On the Self-Exposure of Faith to the Modern Secular World: Philosophical Reflections in Light of Jewish Experience," *Daedalus*, XCVI, No. 1, p. 197.

those brothers and friends, men and women, who did not find easy access into their existing churches but who nevertheless took responsibility for the situation: modest and humble scientists, defeated politicians and desperate soldiers, those involved in the conspiracy against Hitler, and others. Bonhoeffer, the churchman and the theologian, was among them.

For those whom Bonhoeffer labelled "us," there was the need to rediscover the biblical Christ without the religious bonds and outer garments. In whom was man to believe? Bonhoeffer pointed to the Christ who destroyed previous conditions and pre-accepted doctrines for faith; the Christ who made his life his prayer and not half-hearted religious acts; the Christ who did not escape into a *Deus-ex-machina* religion; the Christ who parted himself from the privileged ones and ate with the outcasts; the Christ who by his defenselessness freed man for his own responsibilities, delivering him from patronizing powers.

Bonhoeffer's quest for "Christ today" always went in the direction of the earthly Jesus of the Sermon on the Mount, the man of the cross—which emphasized the revolutionary element—more than it leaned toward metaphysical doctrines of God which would usually have involved him in giving support to the already present establishments.

The quest was somewhat pretentious but all the more significant. "The 'religious act' is always something partial; 'faith' is something whole, involving the whole of one's life. Jesus calls men, not to a new religion, but to life" (LP 199).

59

Observations on Bonhoeffer's Use of Christological Titles

The particular character of Bonhoeffer's life question, "Who is Christ for us today?" makes it clear how his christological utterances can sound so traditional and yet so provocative. What is this Christology like?

His Christology maintains its roots in the classical notions of the ecumenical creeds. In worship, confession, apologetics, teaching, and everyday conversation, we find him using the wide range of christological titles found in both the New Testament and in the Fathers.

Firstly, one finds him worshiping Christ with the ecumenical formulas of the great liturgies and with the personal pietistic and subjective names for Jesus found in his German hymnbook. In this fashion he prayed *to* Christ until the end of his life, whether in the pew of a church or in his prison cell.

Secondly, one finds Bonhoeffer battling for Christ publicly wherever he finds His image vitally distorted. Out of a sudden barrage of quotations from the old confessions of his church he was able to build protective walls for the sufferers of humanity against the destroyers of humanity. Jesus, the Christ of the Old and the New Testament, was made, in spite of a certain doctrinal repetitiousness, the source of a most relevant battle-cry: "Jesus is a Jew." Thus Bonhoeffer confessed *for* Christ, battling in synods and periodicals for the old titles as legal and legitimate formulas against heresy.

One finds, thirdly, in Bonhoeffer's teaching, whether

it be about the early councils or about Melanchthon's deviation into soteriology, his doctrinal defense of the decisions of the Fathers against their contemporary heresies. Thus he teaches *about* Christ in the lecture room.

And fourthly, we find in his conversations with friends inside and outside of church circles his description of Jesus of Nazareth. This description takes form both in those christological titles which do justice to Him and preserve the necessary continuity with the Fathers, and in terms which uncover his centrality afresh for the present day. Here Bonhoeffer is risking Christ for his love for Christ and for his contemporaries. He speaks *of* Christ.

This is the full aspect of Bonhoeffer's use of christological titles. In the vocative of prayer and hymns, in the polemic statement of combat, in his teaching of the church's confessions and in the daring interpretations of present dialogue, he used the titles in a wide range, encompassing both what was accepted objective dogma yet also including lesser-known titles of his own invention. He never renounced or repudiated the titles he inherited; but he read, applied, and selected them in his own way, and went so far as to offer a new one.

Characteristics of Bonhoeffer's Christology

Presuming that the drive which lead Bonhoeffer to the last formula of "non-religious interpretation" was at work all his life, one can detect four features which characterize Bonhoeffer's Christology. First, he wanted to get away from *speculative* descriptions of the natures of Christ; second, he interpreted the traditional christological formulas *relationally;* third, he claimed that all reality was *universally* Christ-centered; and fourth, Christology is fundamentally an *open* and ever unfinished task, living in new responses to the challenge of the encounter with Christ and the world.

Antispeculative. Bonhoeffer was an admirer of the decision of Chalcedon. He defended its wisdom in not reconciling the paradoxes and its witness to the person of the God-man Jesus Christ. The decisive notion of Christ's being the "person" was explicitly developed by Bonhoeffer as early as *Sanctorum Communio* and *Act and Being.*

> [Chalcedon] stated the *a priori* impossibility and impermissibility of taking the divinity and humanity in Jesus Christ side by side or together or as a relationship of objectifiable entities. Simple negations remain. No positive pattern of thought is left to explain what happens in the God-man Jesus Christ. . . . It brings the concept of substance which underlies the relationship of the natures to a climax and does away with it. From now on it will no longer be permissible to say anything about the *substance* of Jesus Christ. Speculation about 'natures' is at an end; the notion of substance is superseded (CC 91–92).

Therefore the problem of Christology for Bonhoeffer is not "the relationship of an isolated God to an isolated man" but the relationship of the given God-man Jesus Christ to the world (CC 46, 108). He thus does not reflect so much on the incarnation as such, but on the humiliation of the Incarnate. At the scandalous ambiguity of a humiliated Jesus, Bonhoeffer wrote that man shall "point and say he is God," this being Luther's battle-cry to which Bonhoeffer refers again and again. "In the humiliation, Christ . . . goes incognito as a beggar among beggars, as an outcast among the outcast, despairing among the despairing, dying among the dying. . . . And here the central problem of Christology lies" (CC 111).

It is not in a "metaphysical" realm but in the person of Christ that man is faced with real and afflicting transcendence; his given person is impenetrable, inaccessible, being-free-from-others and being-for-others, opening himself to others. In his lectures of 1933 Bonhoeffer dismisses, therefore, all speculative questions which try to break open the Logos-Christ and reduce the personal element in Him to metaphysical substances and His transcendence to immanent classification.

> There is in fact only one question left: "Who are you? Speak!" The question "Who are you?" is the question of deposed, distraught reason. But it is equally the question of faith: Who are you? Are you God himself? This is the question with which Christology is concerned. Christ is the Anti-Logos. There is no longer any possibility of classification because the existence of this Logos means the end of the human Logos. The question "Who are you?" is the only appropriate question (CC 30).

All those questions are based on the one which is forbidden: "*How* can you be the Christ?" This Bonhoeffer calls the godless question, the question of immanence.

Though Bonhoeffer's presuppositions in these lectures —the person and the transcendence of the personal, human Logos and Anti-Logos, God—seem to be speculative, he would have nevertheless protested against that charge, because he developed his "speculations" for one reason, viz., to ask the all-important non-speculative question based on the *extra me* and bearing the full *pro me*:

> The only possible meaningful question is, "Who is present and contemporaneous with us here?" The answer is, "The one person of the God-man Jesus Christ." . . . God in timeless eternity is not God, Jesus limited by time is not Jesus. Rather, God is God in the man Jesus. In this Jesus Christ God is present. This one God-man is the starting point of Christology (CC 45–46).

This antispeculative quest had led Bonhoeffer to begin his theologizing with the *church* as the given fact of Christ's presence and to continue with his fight for the visible church and its realm in Nazi Germany. For that reason he nearly equated Christology with ecclesiology, and thus produced in 1927 his *Sanctorum Communio* and in 1936 his embarrassing pamphlets about the identity of salvation with membership in the Confessing Church. But at the same time it was his Christology which empowered him for his bitter criticisms of the actual church, to such a degree that near the end, in 1944, nearly all ecclesiology seems to be absorbed by Christology, giving many present-day interpreters reason to translate Bonhoeffer's "religionless Christianity" into mere "churchless Christianity." But this is a wrong conclusion. Bonhoeffer is quite aware that there must be an ecclesiology if there is to be a Christology, that there are always persons, visibly gathered and drawn into the fate of the Christ-person. Christology without ecclesiology is endangered by abstracts. Therefore he wrote in his first theological letter from Tegel, in a positive, not dismissing, way:

> The questions needing answers would surely be: What do a church, a community, a sermon, a liturgy, a Christian life mean in a religionless world? . . . Does the secret discipline or, alternatively the difference (which I have suggested to you before) between penultimate and ultimate take on a new importance here? (LP 153–54).

Relational. Contrary to the view of Melanchthon, Bonhoeffer was of the opinion that "Christology is not soteriology" (CC 37); that the work does not interpret the person, but, as Luther says, the person the works; that the *extra nos* must not be dissolved into the *pro nobis* and that the *pro nobis* rests on the *extra nos;* that the Who-question preserves the priority of the christological question over the soteriological.

This, however, did not mean that there could be any christological statement which would ignore the social and ethical involvements of present-day man in distinctively human communities, in discipleship and worldly participation; Bonhoeffer stated in *Act and Being:* "The extrinsicality of the Christ-person is essentially transcendent of existence, yet it 'is' only in its action on human existence" (p. 139).

Thus the christological answer to the question "Who are You?" would on the one hand create the identity of the Christian as such, but on the other hand would also release him into identification with other persons. It had been Bonhoeffer's first thesis in *Sanctorum Com-*

munio that there are no theological *loci* which lack the element of sociality. It is the same quest for relational sociality that led Bonhoeffer in 1927 to describe Christ as "existing as church"—church primarily meaning the fellowship of persons and not the institution; the same quest that made him give precedence to the present Christ over the historical Christ in the lectures from 1933; that in 1935 turned Christology into a fellowship of men who hear a call and respond; that in Christ's name put man into worldly responsibility. Thus in the *Ethics* of 1940 and finally in the self-identifying suffering of 1944 he could have said what he had earlier written:

> Discipleship means adherence to Christ, and, because Christ is the object of that adherence, it must take the form of discipleship. An abstract Christology, a doctrinal system, a general religious knowledge on the subject of grace or on the forgiveness of sins, render discipleship superfluous, and in fact they positively exclude any idea of discipleship whatever, and are essentially inimical to the whole conception of following Christ. . . . Christianity without the living Christ is inevitably Christianity without discipleship, and Christianity without discipleship is always Christianity without Christ (CD 63–64).

Universal. Compared with Teilhard de Chardin's cosmological interests, Bonhoeffer's thinking and feelings circled primarily around persons and their history, relations, and responsibilities. There is in him, nevertheless, a strong tendency to expand the centrality of Christ into universal, perhaps ontological, claims. The category of the Person (the Christ-person) provided him with a means by which man and Christ were united, but it also offered him the centerpoint, around which everything else gained perspective and enlightenment. As in previous theologies and as in the New Testament—see, for instance, the development to the secondary Pauline letters—the personal, revealing encounter led to the discovery of cosmological and historical dimensions; in classical dogmatic terms, reconciliation was followed by the vision of redemption (*Versöhnung-Erlösung*). In 1932 Bonhoeffer developed in *Creation and Fall* and in his other writings a type of Colossian cosmological Christology. In 1933 he stated that the Christ-presence *pro nobis* means His being in the center of all human existence, of history and of nature. The ungraspable but self-revealing person of Christ the Lord is in Bonhoeffer's proclamation not only the limiting boundary, but also the sustaining power of all reality.

In the *Ethics* Bonhoeffer shows again the ultimate unity of all reality in Christ; there is no reality without God in Christ; and there is no God in Christ without the reality; otherwise Christ or reality remain abstractions. Christ is not absolute reality *added* to worldly reality, nor is reality just material, onto which Christ, Christian programs, or ideals are forced. The unity of all reality in Christ is not synthetic, not magical, but real and made valid by the Christ, the redeemer and vicarious deputy.

It is from the real man, whose name is Jesus Christ, that all factual reality derives its ultimate foundation and its ultimate annulment, its justification and its ultimate contradiction, its ultimate affirmation and its ultimate negation (E 228).

There are . . . not two spheres, but only the one sphere of the realization of Christ, in which the reality of God and the reality of the world are united (E 197).

. . . It is only in the midst of the world that Christ is Christ (E 206).

There is in Bonhoeffer a tendency to express the "onto-logical" universal centrality of Christ in anthropological terms—so in one of his last letters he said, "If this earth was good enough for the man Jesus Christ, if such a man as Jesus lived in it, then, and only then, has life a meaning for us" (LP 214). Heinrich Ott is certainly right in *Wirklichkeit und Glaube* when he states that this notion of total reality-penetration by the Christ-event is a characteristic motif of Bonhoeffer's thought. Perhaps Ott has not shown clearly enough the danger of ontologization which usually results in clericalization of the world, leading, in turn, to the unbalancing of the proper relation of a *theologia gloriae* with the *theologia crucis,* where the crucified Lord is the triumphant center and the triumphant one is the Crucified. But Ott is basically right: Bonhoeffer could also say in Tegel, "In the facts, there is God." The structure of this universalistic Christology, however, is basically not unhistoric ontology, for it is structured by the very notion of reconciliation and of ongoing, dynamic "acceptance."

Open. At the end of his prison letters Bonhoeffer proposed his answer to the question, "Who is Christ for us today?" He speaks in the outline for a book (August, 1944) about the God-encounter in the encounter with Christ in which there is an inversion (*Umkehrung*) of all human existence, where the genuine experience of transcendence is given in Jesus' being for others:

> God in human form—not, as in oriental religions, in animal form, monstrous, chaotic, remote, and terrifying, nor in the conceptual forms of the absolute, metaphysical, infinite, etc., nor yet in the Greek divine-human form of "man in himself," but "the man for others," and therefore the Crucified, the man who lives out of the transcendent (LP 210).

"Jesus, the man for others" is in fact a new christological title for Bonhoeffer. It is nothing less than an answer to his over-arching question; for it is faithful to the tradition, non-speculative, relational, and central for all being and reality. The answer is as simple as it is profound, as understandable as it is sophisticated, as anthropological as it is theological. This christological title fulfills four essential requirements: that of continuity, that of being theological, that of being existential, and that of having ethical implications.

(1) Continuity. Sociality had been a leading concept of Bonhoeffer's since *Sanctorum Communio*. The Lutheran *pro me* was always central, yet counterbalanced against any individualistic narrowness. The *extra me* was always sought by Bonhoeffer in the transcendence of the Christ-person, where he found transcendence to be relevant, terribly near and tantalizingly far away. His idea of the "man for others" could be traced to his basic concepts about the vicarious deputyship of Jesus' participation in God's powerlessness, and His interceding suffering. In this way this title of Jesus was for Bonhoeffer a more "majestic title" (*Hoheitstitel*) than some of the old ones, such as "King" or "Son."

(2) Theological. This christological title was for Bonhoeffer strictly theological, expressing something about God more convincingly than many of the older revered ones. The passage just cited (LP 210) begins not with a reduction but with the claim to interpret "God," yet "in human form." Such a statement uncovers the real godlessness and guilt of man in an act which put him to shame, yet liberated and claimed him with new grace. Medieval man was either shamed or lifted up by royal imagery; his life depended on the nature of his king, yet he visualized the ideal king. Today, however, the royal image is relegated to the historical dramas at the Old Vic or to Disneyland, and with it its theological claim.

(3) Existential. The theological statement must include an assertion about human existence. Its relevance reaches not only the inner circles of the church, but the "world" as well. It is related to everyday reality and uncovers the center of creativity for today. It has no false connotations of exclusiveness for initiated groups who claim possession of certain mysteries, although the most unmysterious dimension, "being for others," *is* the actual mystery of life. It means that the mystery of Christ's uniqueness is his being for others. This *is* his true uniqueness, viz., he has no interest in his own uniqueness. The anthropological character of the title *is* its theological essence.

The history of this title may be similar to the classical titles which came before it. The christological marriage between the person of Christ and relevant existential names is the result of a discernible courtship. One first seeks to acquaint himself with the nature of the title as such—lamb, shepherd, king, or man for others—but by coupling it to Christ, it becomes clear that one really did not know the true meaning of the terms. Finally the title begins to be corrected and filled with in its true content by Christ himself. Thus, as with the old titles long ago, christological meaning penetrates the anthropological, and anthropological meaning the christological.

(4) Ethical. This term at once unleashes ethical implications and involvements. It takes Christ out of the fairy-tale world and locates him in the context of the present pluralistic responsibilities of man come of age. It liberates human existence for new freedom and obedience. The character of the new title prohibits any flight from the world, and also excludes clerical or ecclesiastical world dominance.

The ethical simplicity of the title points to the actual costliness of its use; it rules out what Bonhoeffer had earlier called uninvolved "cheap grace," and it abhors the contemporary purely intellectual "God-talk" game. The title renews the *imitatio Christi*.

This title, saturated with Bonhoeffer's own experiences, praises Christ *today*, interprets his meaning, and confesses him before men of our time. In our attempt to understand the nature of a "non-religious interpretation of biblical concepts in a world come of age," we find an example in Bonhoeffer's last christological answer of what such a program might be: non-metaphysical, non-individualistic, non-sectorial, against the establishment of religious privileges, against the *Deus ex machina*, and against guardianship.

Of course Bonhoeffer's title for Christ lacks the second feature of general christological titles: acceptance by the universal church. But next to the received classical titles, one must acknowledge the existence of a wide range of personal titles, created through the centuries, sometimes received in our hymnbooks, differing in quality and strength, but all attempting to delineate a contemporary understanding of the Christ-person. Bonhoeffer's proposal, until now only a proposal, is offered to us as the culmination of intensive intellectual wrestling, committed prayer, and acting intercourse with the question, "Who is Christ for us today?"

Men go to God when they are sore bestead,
Pray to him for succour, for his peace, for bread,
For mercy for them sick, sinning or dead;
All men do so, Christian and unbelieving.

Men go to God when he is sore bestead,
Find him poor and scorned, without shelter or bread,
Whelmed under weight of the wicked, the weak, the dead;
Christians stand by God in his hour of grieving.

God goeth to every man when sore bestead,
Feedeth body and spirit with his bread;
For Christians, pagans alike he hangeth dead,
And both alike forgiving.[7]

---

[7] "Christians and Pagans," LP 200.

TURNING POINTS IN BONHOEFFER'S LIFE AND THOUGHT

by Eberhard Bethge

I

Bonhoeffer's name and some of his catch phrases have by now crossed the boundaries of his confession, the Lutheran church, and his native land, Germany. This has happened despite, or perhaps because of, the veil of incognito under which his life ended in 1945.

The "incognito" of his death in the extermination camp at Flossenburg was so complete that only after long months of anxiety was his family able to obtain information as to when and where it took place. For the executioners, their victim had no name other than the label "Enemy of the State." Thus he was "extinguished," as the officials of that time expressed it, nameless like millions of Jews, his ashes thrown into the wind. There was no funeral, no sermon. And today there is no grave where reverence can make up for what was denied at the time of chaos.

But the incognito of time and place extends beyond Bonhoeffer's personal existence. It also affects what he stood for. Of course, he wanted to become effective: "[sometimes] there comes over me a longing (unlike any other that I experience) not to vanish without a trace" (LP 107). But exactly for that reason he accepted, like his family and his friends, the risk of anonymity and incognito. First, he was not allowed to preach or to publish in his own country. Then he gave up the relative prominence which his church could still offer him. Thus his final decision and all that followed was wrapped in silence. The very nature of that decision allowed no previous discussion or vindication. His theological students and colleagues in the church for a long time remained in ignorance of Bonhoeffer's final steps and conclusion, and they were deeply surprised when the true character of those steps gradually came to light.

Many were actually left nearly helpless in face of both the facts and the verbal expressions which Bonhoeffer gave in the prison letters. The usual dogmatic concepts seemed to submerge, the usual formulations of Protestant ethics no longer seemed to fit. The image of a Christian martyr no longer seemed compatible with the new facts, at any rate not within the tradition of German Lutheranism.

As early as 1945, Bonhoeffer's own church in Berlin-Brandenburg stood aloof from its former pastor whose image had become obscure. In a solemn declaration by the newly established church government on the occasion of the first anniversary of the attempted assassination of Hitler on July 20, 1944, Dietrich Bonhoeffer's name was not mentioned, while Pastor Paul Schneider from the village of Dickenschied, who from his simple refusal to obey the Gestapo was beaten to death in 1939, was pronounced "a martyr in the fullest sense of the word." This declaration made a revealing distinction when it informed the congregations of the church "that this church could never approve of the plot of July 20, 1944, whatever its purpose may have been, and that amongst those who have suffered in consequence were countless persons who never wished this attempted assassination to take place."

A little later, in 1948, in the German town of Bielefeld, certain streets were to be renamed in memory of members of the German resistance movement. Local pastors, however, sought to prevent the names of their fellow clergy from appearing together with those of socialists and atheists who were part of the resistance. They wrote to Dietrich Bonhoeffer's father: "A number of names have been chosen of men who became victims of National Socialism, among them Paul Schneider (Dickenschied) and your son Dietrich. We, the pastors of this town, have grave misgivings about the choice of both these names, as we should not like the names of our fellow pastors who died for their faith to appear side by side with political martyrs." The Berlin church did not quite know how to deal with Dietrich Bonhoeffer, this dissident member. The pastors of Bielefeld clearly wanted to keep their fellow clergy neatly to themselves.

Today after more than twenty years something has changed, but something has also remained the same. The phenomenon of Bonhoeffer's actions and the conclusions he reached before his death are still not clarified or integrated.

Recently, the council of a large German regional church has forbidden one of its parishes to name a newly built church after Bonhoeffer. And some years

ago a bishop of standing refused to attend the dedication of a memorial tablet in Flossenburg where Bonhoeffer's death-camp was located, on the grounds that
it carried the name of a—so the bishop wrote—"political,
not a Christian martyr."

Such are the difficulties of Christian churches with one
of their members. Much more tantalizing, however, are
the barriers to understanding which come from the side
of those for whom Bonhoeffer's decision was made and
his risks run. The Jewish philosopher Emil L. Fackenheim wrote recently in reflection upon Bonhoeffer's idea
of modern man come of age:

> Clear-sighted witness, apostle of Christian self-exposure to
> the secular world, and himself a martyr to his cause, Bon-
> hoeffer nevertheless failed wholly to grasp . . . the monstrous
> evil in the actual world about him. This painful truth, in
> retrospect inescapable, cannot escape his Jewish reader. In
> a concentration camp filled with Jews subjected to every
> imaginable form of torture, Bonhoeffer writes that Protes-
> tants must learn about suffering from Catholics. No mention
> is made in the letters and papers from prison of Jewish
> martyrdom.[1]

Fackenheim probably reads Bonhoeffer's analysis of
modern man in the isolated perspective of current and
optimistic American theologians who have taken up the
term "modern man" as pointing to a man—as Fackenheim
says—"happy in his secularity and free of guilt." Such
commentators, before whom we as Germans hesitate to
justify ourselves after Auschwitz, make us forget the con-

[1] Emil L. Fackenheim, "On the Self-Exposure of Faith to the
Modern Secular World: Philosophical Reflections in Light of Jewish
Experience," *Daedalus,* Journal of the American Academy of Arts
and Sciences, XCVI, No. 1, p. 197. Quoted by permission of the
publisher.

text of Bonhoeffer's theological writings and actual situation. Bonhoeffer's words about man come of age, which never meant that man had become better but rather more adult and therefore more responsible, stand in strong dialectical relation to his words about partaking in God's suffering on earth (LP 197). Furthermore he had written a confession of guilt long before the church confessed this in 1945. He wrote in 1940 that the church "was silent when she should have cried out because the blood of the innocent was crying aloud to heaven. . . . She is guilty of the deaths of the weakest and most defenceless brothers of Jesus Christ" (E 113–14). When he began to develop his ideas about secularity in the *Ethics* in 1942 he wrote a chapter under the heading "The Acceptance of Guilt" as well.

Finally, Bonhoeffer's church struggle from 1933 onward had its very center in his fight against the "Aryan clause," not in a fight for the self-preservation of the church. The Bonhoeffer family, with four of their men in prison, risked their lives in order to put an end to the incredible sufferings of the Jews. How then could Dietrich in his years of active plotting have written statements about the Jews in letters which were smuggled out of prison while his friends outside were working to bring about the plot? Should, by chance, the letters have been discovered one could possibly have covered up statements about "Catholics," but never about Jews.

Thus, Bonhoeffer's own church is still fostering doubts about his martyrdom because it is not able to understand his presupposition whereby martyrdom is combined with identification with others in unsaintly guilt. And the contemporary Jewish commentator limits that martyrdom to an irrelevant concept of untainted sanctity because he is not aware of the conscious dimension of guilt in Bonhoeffer's death. Neither acknowledges his mature way of identification with both the guilty and the victims. But that identification did indeed take place.

Bonhoeffer himself expected that the path he had chosen would threaten the customary standards of his church. He wrote in one of the smuggled letters that he was aware that his path, once known, might well "endanger the exercise of my vocation later on" (WE 118). But he knew as well that he could not turn for approval to those authorities which had previously allowed those accepted ethical standards to be riven asunder by the events of history in such an irresponsible and bloodstained way. He also wrote from his cell: "I became certain that the duty had been laid on me to hold out in this boundary situation with all its problems; I became quite content to do this, and have remained so ever since" (LP 87). . . . [From 1940 until now] I knew quite well what I was doing, and I acted with a clear conscience. . . . And I regard my being kept here . . . as being involved in the part that I had resolved to play in Germany's fate. It is with no reproach that I look back on the past and accept the present" (LP 115).

II

A solution to the enigma of Bonhoeffer's life and thought may be approached by looking at two turning points along his way. The first may have occurred about

78

1931-32 and might be formulated thus: Dietrich Bonhoeffer the theologian became a Christian. The second began in 1939: Dietrich Bonhoeffer the Christian became a contemporary, a man of his own particular time and place.

Both sound obvious, but in fact they were not at all so. The sequence is what matters and the combination is rare. Indeed, it does not often happen that a theologian, a Christian, and a man of his time appear in a conscious and molded way in the same person. In Bonhoeffer's case the steps he took each time to combine intellectual expertness (the theologian) with life-engagement (the Christian) and finally with unreserved presence (the contemporary) brought about immense changes in his way of living and writing. Each step by itself might have sufficed to give content to a man's activity, but the two had to combine to chisel out his life's work, and both together make his name what it is for us now.

For the first turning point we possess much evidence regarding the obvious results. This evidence shows how the young theologian engaged himself in a disciplined churchlife which was quite unfamiliar to his family and to his theological teachers. But as far as the turning point itself is concerned, its motives and the time and circumstances of its occurrence, we are virtually without genuine sources. Bonhoeffer never said a thing about when he may have undergone some kind of personal conversion. He did not even like the term "conversion"; his upbringing forbade such language and his theological outlook was accustomed to fighting against such self-analysis. We may only observe that there he went through continuing unrest during his years of intense theological writing and that this was followed by a growing certainty of his vocation and working out of his own concepts which replaced the wavering of direction. This turning certainly took months and years to reach maturity; but once he did express in a letter to a girl to whom he was attached that there was a definite end and a new beginning. The letter was written in the winter of 1935/36 and may have referred to a period in 1931 when Bonhoeffer took up his career as a teacher and a pastor. In the letter he said:

I hurled myself into my work in an unchristian and unhumble manner. . . . Then something else came along, something which has permanently changed my life and its direction. . . . I had often preached, I had seen a lot of the church, I had talked and written about it, but I had not yet become a Christian. (I know that until then I had been using the cause of Jesus Christ to my own advantage. . . .)

The Bible, most particularly the Sermon on the Mount, has freed me from all this. Since then everything has changed. . . . I now realized that the life of a servant of Jesus Christ must belong to the church, and step by step it became clearer to me to what extent this must be so.

Then came the distress of 1933. That strengthened my conviction. And then too I found others ready to concentrate their attention on this goal. All that mattered to me was the renewal of the church and of the pastoral profession. . . .

Christian pacifism, which I had attacked passionately until shortly before, suddenly revealed itself as a matter of course. . . . My vocation lies before me. What God will make of it, I do not know. . . .

I believe we shall only perceive the gloriousness of this vocation in the times to come and the events they will bring.
If only we can hold out.

Bonhoeffer never said such things to anyone except
in this confessional letter. None in his family would
have observed any drastic change. His students, however, who from now on came into contact with him, became aware of his personal involvement with his subject
matter and his obvious yet unobtrusive practical discipline of prayer. When Bonhoeffer, just turned twenty-
five, began lecturing at Berlin University in the winter
of 1931/32, his students formed themselves into a closer
circle and found him familiarizing them with such un-
modern ideas as the possibility of leading a community
life in study and prayer. We now know how new this
was for Bonhoeffer himself. It was strange and startling
to hear of such "Catholicizing" tendencies by a theologian whose teaching was based strictly on Reformation theology, and later to find such ideas put into
practice. But many realized that here theology did not
continue to be merely uncommitted research or a mental
exercise, not the display of a rearguard action of apologetic argument, but rather the deploying of Christian
understanding with triumphant self-confidence.

When the gales of 1933 swept over the universities,
and many theological faculties, weak by their lack of
commitment and crippled by their relationship to the
state, fell victim to the National Socialist policy of
eliminating opposition, Bonhoeffer and his little group
stuck to their posts in Berlin University unaffected by
the lure of the so-called "Springtime of Germany." But

in the autumn of that year he gave up his academic career in anger and shame, determined to remain a theologian only in the service of the opposing Confessing Church. This, of course, could give no promise of a career.

Who was this man who as a theologian now vigorously chose also to be a committed Christian?

Bonhoeffer was the son of a large German upper-class family, his father being the leading psychiatrist at Berlin University; there were four brothers and four sisters. At his birth no one would have prophesied that he would become a theologian and a parson, the prevailing interests in his home having been medicine, natural science, and law, and music dominant among the arts. During his schooldays Dietrich's parents encouraged his love of music, for he showed signs of becoming a first-rate pianist. But when in the next to last year of gymnasium, at the age of fifteen, he was required to choose another old or new language for study, he took Hebrew which signaled his final decision to study theology.

When on one occasion his brothers—all older than he —teased him about his intention of entering the church, which they thought "nothing but a relic for philistine, bourgeois, and backward minds," the young boy answered defiantly, "Well, then I shall reform that church." The church did not count for much in the Bonhoeffer home in Berlin-Grunewald even though they adhered to Christian ethics and observed some Christian customs. But even Dietrich's mind was not much set on the church at first. To him it seemed more worth-while to become a theologian than a parson and to deal in that way with other people's philosophies and agnosticism. With this passionate desire he began to study theology, beginning energetically with epistemology according to Kant and sociology according to Max Weber. When he was nineteen and already in his third year of study, he was spellbound by the theology of the early Karl Barth, whom he did not meet until much later. His great teachers on the Berlin faculty, Adolf von Harnack, Karl Holl, and Reinhold Seeberg, anxiously watched the gifted student leaving the fold and turning his back on the accepted course in order, as they thought, to surrender to the Barthian concept, the facile theology of the preached word. But although Bonhoeffer remained attracted by the latter, because he sensed that there theology was once again coming to recognize its own true right and value, he nevertheless treated his distant master, Barth, with the same independence he showed toward his teachers near at hand.

At twenty-one he finished his thesis for his doctorate, *Sanctorum Communio*, a discussion of the sociological and theological character of the church, and at twenty-four he gained access to the lecturing desk of Berlin University by way of an essay on *Act and Being*, a highly modern treatment of the tension between Barthian transcendentalism and traditional ontologism. These writings prove Bonhoeffer to have been a theologian of precise argument, able to move with sovereign ease in two fields of theology, liberal criticism and the "theology of crisis." In both fields he put questions to the great authorities and even ventured to suggest new solutions. In point of fact he revealed himself to be one who never acknowledged exclusive alternatives, seeking rather a way to overcome the deadlock. Thus he was generally regarded as a theologian equipped with excellent qualifications and well on the way to a chair at one of the German theological faculties.

He began to be tormented, however, by the question of whether a chair in a theological faculty with its attendant state privileges could still be a place from which he could hope to reveal the independent mystery of the Christian message and make it relevant and comprehendible. Wavering, he looked for the simple ministry. To his eldest brother, the physicist, he wrote: "It is queer how hard it is to make up one's mind. . . . The question is how to combine the function of parson with university teaching. For I think I mustn't give that up" (GS III, 24).

It was not a year until he "gave that up." A decision was made and the disquiet had been overcome. In the meantime, to be sure, circumstances had changed; therefore he even declined a ministry in Berlin, because, since 1933, such an office could only be obtained after submission to the Aryan clause. He accepted the small ministry to Germans in London. From there he wrote, to Erwin Sutz in Switzerland, about teaching theology in a way which astonishes us because we know his later and different utterances about exposing theology to the attacks of modern science. But at that time his words were proper answers to the threat against freedom and independence, revealing how the old places of binding and fettering research had suddenly become the only places of real freedom.

I no longer have any faith in the university, in fact I have never really had any—much to their annoyance. The whole training of the coming generation of theology students ought to take place in monastery schools in which Christ's true teaching, the Sermon on the Mount, and the right form of worship are taken seriously. This is not done with regard to any of these three things at the university and it is impossible under existing circumstances. And at long last a stop must be put to that reticence on would-be theological grounds concerning the actions of the state—it is in fact due simply to fear. "Open thy mouth for the dumb." Who in the church today acknowledges that this is the very least of the demands the Bible makes on us in these times? (GS I, 42).

The Confessing Church, which was robbed of the usual privileges of the church, invited him in 1935 to the preacher's seminar at Finkenwalde. There Bonhoeffer again took up theology joyfully, but now in a closed circle of "brethren." He told his eldest brother: "When I began to study theology I imagined it was something quite different, I daresay a more academic affair. But now at last I feel certain that for once, at least, I have landed on the right track—for the first time in my life. And that often makes me very happy" (GS III, 25).

This first turning point changed Bonhoeffer's way of life gradually and left deep traces. The center of his living moved more and more beyond his parents' home. In 1935 and 1936 he could say to a group of his students: "Don't go home for Christmas; it is not primarily a family feast, but a celebration of the church community." Every branch of his theological research now included visible ecclesiastical involvement.

The true product of all this was to be found in the two books which during his lifetime bore for interested theologians and churchmen the stamp of Bonhoeffer's personality, *The Cost of Discipleship* and *Life Together*. Like a fanfare of trumpets the first chapters of the first of these books remained in the reader's ear: the church is poisoning itself by its use of cheap grace. Here was not the pious soul just outside or on the fringe of the church, but a theologian within the church itself and dedicated to the theology of justification by faith, who stated in embarrassing equation: "Only he who believes is obedient, and only he who is obedient believes" (CD 69). In his two earlier books, written at Berlin University, he had still spoken in foreign tongues and with borrowed ideas which makes them such difficult reading. In these two books, however, he speaks his own language. They made a distinctive contribution to the history of Lutheran theology and to the piety of his church. *The Cost of Discipleship* was immediately read not only by theological specialists but also by laymen. Even today many great theologians, including Karl Barth, consider this book to be by far Bonhoeffer's greatest achievement.

This turning point brought Bonhoeffer, furthermore, into a community of brethren in Finkenwalde who, joining him in the battles against the compromising church authorities, led a life of disciplined worship. This brought about the founding of the so-called *Bruderhaus,* House of Brethren, a kind of precursor to the communities formed since by Protestants in some areas of the ecumenical movement, such as at Taizé, Sicily, Imshausen and Darmstadt. For Bonhoeffer, according to the testimony of his own writings, his time at Finkenwalde was the most profitably filled time of his life to that point, speaking both professionally and humanly (GS II, 458).

This turning point thus involved the Confessing Church, Finkenwalde, and *The Cost of Discipleship*. But it also meant an uncompromising resistance to the National Socialist regime and its church policy right from the beginning and the building up of a society of a few men who were prepared to rush to the places of emergency in the ongoing battles. That was the salt which seasoned everything and prevented Finkenwalde and the "life together" from turning into self-introverted ideals. It even kept them open for new and different developments.

Bonhoeffer had long reckoned with being led on the way that ended as Paul Schneider ended in 1939; or on the way where one of the very few German conscientious objectors, Hermann Stoehr, came to death in 1940. But the course of his life moved gradually on to a new dimension. A mutation was beginning which confirmed what Bonhoeffer once, in 1932, predicted, when he preached in Berlin, and when—without fully realizing its implications and its real shape—he said that the blood of martyrs might once again be demanded, but "this blood, if we really have the courage and loyalty to shed it, will not be innocent, shining like that of the first witnesses for the faith. On our blood lies heavy guilt, the guilt of the unprofitable servant who is cast into outer darkness" (GS IV, 71).

III

With this we have moved to the second turning point, which brought with it a second impact on Bonhoeffer's way of life and consequently on his theology.

Once again it bore fruit in two books. But they remained incomplete, since they appeared posthumously. They did, however, carry Bonhoeffer's name into the world: *Ethics* and the collection, *Letters and Papers from Prison.*

This second turning point also led him into a group of fellow workers and like-minded men. But this circle was different and in a way both more wide and more limited at the same time. He again joined his own brothers in their political efforts and found himself among comrades who knew little of his Finkenwalde associates. They were a circle of conspirators working to put down injustice and—if possible—to create a new Germany. For the brothers at Finkenwalde a veil began to shroud a part of Bonhoeffer's way of life and they did not dare to question him about it. Conversely, his life in a Christian community was not clearly perceived by the new associates. Yet there was no impression of a man torn between two ideals. All was of a piece. The dimly suspected depth of the background made him the more intriguing.

Nevertheless, the new turning point gradually demanded its own new sacrifice, the sacrifice of his reputation as a Christian minister. It transported him from a relatively clear world where the choice was simply between confessing and denying, a Yes or a No, into an ambiguous world where expedients, tactics and camouflage, success and failure, all had to be carefully calculated. Once, in 1932, he had found his place in the church and his vocation gained its certainty. Now he was searching for his place in the world and his destiny consisted of nothing but preliminary factors. There grew up around his friends and himself the loneliness of the men of action who no longer can seek justification from outside but must leave that to God alone.

Not until now did Dietrich Bonhoeffer, the theologian and Christian, enter fully into the present condition of his particular time and place. As a member of the upper bourgeois world which until then had not done very much actively to prevent the Nazi-condition from coming about, he accepted the whole weight of this class's responsibility for that condition. With his brothers and friends who were ready to pay the price of atonement, he took upon himself the burden of overcoming this state of affairs instead of merely making further ideological protests from the pulpit.

This second turning point, which only gradually took its own shape so that old and new elements often overlap and intertwine, had a rather exact date when it began to assume its new direction. We know now that Bonhoeffer spent the hot evening of June 19, 1939, walking up and down Times Square, New York, painfully aware that he had to make a final decision the next morning. He had come to America in order to leave Germany and his own dilemma behind. He had allowed himself to be carried away by the disappointments of

1938, the most disastrous year in the Nazi period for his church. In that year everything had reached a climax. The resistance to the state church by pastors and his candidates for the ministry had grown weaker and weaker. Almost all the pastors of the Confessing Church, together with neutral and "Teutonic Christian" ministers had taken an impossibly comprehensive and unconditioned oath of loyalty to Hitler. In the face of the so-called "crystal night," i.e., the destruction of the Jewish synagogues all over Germany by the storm-troopers, even his oppositional Confessing Church had remained silent. A first real attempt at a *putsch* against Hitler, in which Bonhoeffer's brother-in-law Hans von Dohnanyi had taken a decisive part, had miscarried because of Hitler's victorious reception of Chamberlain, Daladier, and Mussolini at the Munich Conference. Nothing could be done now to stop the war for which his country was blatantly preparing. He was himself likely soon to be conscripted for military service and the Confessing Church wanted by all means to avoid another fatal clash with the authorities which would come if its prominent member Bonhoeffer might refuse to serve. A good solution presented itself in Bonhoeffer's leaving the country, at least for a while. Lastly his own large family had been disrupted in 1938 by the sudden forced emigration of his twin sister and her family, an emigration brought about by the Non-Aryan legislation.

Had he not every right now to abandon this Germany and this Church? Was it not permissible for him to live on safer grounds in order to pursue his theological vocation and to write the *Ethics*, which he felt to be his main task in life? Had he not always been part and parcel of the ecumenical movement, which through its American friends had invited him now in order that he should save himself for the future?

It was late that night when Bonhoeffer went home, to his guest room in Union Theological Seminary. On the morning of June 20 he was to sit opposite his helper and guide, Dr. Henry Smith-Leiper, the Secretary of the Federal Council of the Churches of Christ in America. Leiper had collected several thousand dollars for Bonhoeffer's new tasks in America. Leiper was glad to have found Bonhoeffer, as he said, "the right man at the right time" for certain jobs. He knew him well from ecumenical meetings in 1933, 1934, and 1936 where he sided up with Bonhoeffer in the fight for resolutions against the Aryan clause in Germany.

Late at night on June 19 Bonhoeffer wrote in his diary:

> Without news from Germany the whole day, from post to post, waiting in vain. It does not help to get angry and write that sort of letter. . . . I want to know how work is going over there, whether all is well or whether they need me. I want to have some sign from over there before the decisive meeting tomorrow. Perhaps it is a good thing that it has not come (WF 232).

The diary of the next night contains the following note:

> Visit Leiper. The decision has been made. I have refused. They were clearly disappointed, and rather upset. It probably means more for me than I can see at the moment. God alone knows. . . .

91

Today the reading speaks dreadfully harshly of God's incorruptible judgement. He certainly sees how much personal feeling, how much anxiety there is in today's decision, however brave it may seem. The reasons one gives for an action to others and to one's self are certainly inadequate. . . . At the end of the day I can only ask God to give a merciful judgement on today and all its decisions. It is now in his hand (WF 233, 234).

Soon afterward Bonhoeffer wrote to Reinhold Niebuhr, who was particularly shocked at this return to Germany, for it was with him and Paul Lehmann that the whole American journey had been mapped out:

Sitting here in Dr. Coffin's garden I have had the time to think and to pray about my situation and that of my nation and to have God's will for me clarified. I have come to the conclusion that I have made a mistake in coming to America. I must live through this difficult period of our national history with the Christian people of Germany. I will have no right to participate in the reconstruction of Christian life in Germany after the war if I do not share the trials of this time with my people. Christians in Germany will face the terrible alternative of either willing the defeat of their nation in order that Christian civilization may survive, or willing the victory of their nation and thereby destroying our civilization. I know which of these alternatives I must choose, but I cannot make that choice in security (WF 246).

At that first turning point in 1931, the ecumenical movement, which offered him now a safe place for his vocation, had unfolded itself to Bonhoeffer too. At that time that movement had been taken up in Germany by only a small minority and—incredible as it now seems —was attacked and reviled from all sorts of nationalistic quarters of the German Lutheran churches and faculties. When Germany became more and more isolated during the 1930's, Bonhoeffer had stood for ecumenism as a more and more impassioned prophet, proclaiming its priority in spite of growing personal risks. By now, when he might have taken refuge in this movement of the *Una Sancta,* he deliberately excluded himself from it. He perceived clearly that there had come up for him a barrier on the way to being a Christian. In his diary for June 22, 1939, we read:

> . . . a catastrophe here [America] is quite inconceivable, unless it is ordained. But even to be responsible, to have to reproach oneself, for having come out [from Germany] unnecessarily, is certainly crushing. But we cannot part ourselves from our destiny, much less here, outside; . . . It is strange how strongly I have been moved by these particular thoughts in the last few days and how all thoughts about the *Una Sancta* make slow progress (WF 235).[2]

Suddenly it became clear to Bonhoeffer that his priorities had changed place. The *Una Sancta* for which he had yearned was fading away as he came to identify himself with Germany at this evil period in her history, and as he began to pursue his purpose actively and firmly in spite of the ambiguities of his position. The *Una Sancta* could be won back in the future only if it were sacrificed now, and only if one day it could be fully agreed that a man had been a responsible member of his country at this time.

It became clear to Bonhoeffer that to desire to be a

---

[2] A more correct translation of this final phrase would be: ". . . and how all thoughts about the *Una Sancta* meet a barrier."

Christian in a vacuum, not to mention being a disciple away from the particular place to which he belonged, would be to poison again the message of Christ. The possibility of remaining a Christian lay now in the more confined and inglorious course, easily misunderstood, of becoming a full contemporary with his family and friends at their own appointed place.

Thus Bonhoeffer returned in July of 1939 to a Germany bristling with arms. For four years he led a double life, still in comparative freedom. First he continued ministering for almost a year to the Confessing Church in its hole-and-corner existence. Then the building up of political resistance took the upper hand. When conscription put an end to the training of ordinands for the Confessing Church, he himself, having no particular obligations toward a parish, could yield to the entreaties of his brother-in-law to put himself at the disposal of the conspiracy under the cover of the Military Intelligence Service. That Service, which under Canaris' skillful leadership was still independent from the Gestapo, had been for years lodging the conspiracy under its own roof. The steps to be taken in this work for another Germany involved a number of ambiguous technical tasks, where church and ecumene had to serve as camouflage for political goals, and political goals had to serve as pretexts for ecclesiastical links.

Thus Bonhoeffer went to meet his old friend George Bell, Bishop of Chichester, on a highly political mission in Sweden in 1942. Thus he made use of his connections via Dr. Visser 't Hooft in the ecumenical offices in Geneva. Thus he took his share in smuggling a few

Jews out of the country under the strange masquerade of Intelligence employees. Thus he helped to draw up certain memoranda for the political and ecclesiastical future of Germany after an overthrow. When time allowed he continued to work happily on his *Ethics*.

In sharing the logic of a conspiracy, Bonhoeffer, on the one hand, allowed himself to be used as a clergyman, who with the trustworthiness he possessed in the Allied countries could establish contacts which the conspiracy desperately needed. On the other hand, he did not expect any special consideration for his position as a clergyman from the side of the planners in the conspiracy; that would have been to repudiate solidarity with those who, without such ecclesiastical privileges, had to perform the necessary job in increasingly complicated circumstances.

This double life turned finally into a race between the conspiracy and the Gestapo as to who should reach its goal first: the conspiracy running to destroy the Gestapo and the system which made it possible; the Gestapo to win the control over Canaris' Military Intelligence Service—not knowing that by this they actually would desperately affect the conspiracy. Under suspicion of violating certain rules of the Intelligence Service, Bonhoeffer, his brother-in-law, Hans von Dohnanyi, and some friends were arrested; but all suspicions were still unprovable. In prison the main point at issue was by all possible diversions to shield the friends who were continuing to act outside. This was successful until the complex plotting came to light after the failure of the attempt on Hitler's life on July 20, 1944.

The character of Bonhoeffer's imprisonment made the veil shrouding his existence still more impenetrable for his church. The actual significance of the decision to return in June, 1939, was not known to his ecclesiastical superiors. The Confessing Church did not include the name of this pastor under military arrest on the intercession list circulated in its parishes. Nothing was seen or known of the full facts of the case and the Confessing Church was not in a position to identify itself publicly with those who suffered for political reasons. Thus the wall of silence around Bonhoeffer grew higher and higher.

In a literary fragment composed in his cell at Tegel, Bonhoeffer makes the main character say:

> What man of goodwill can nowadays bring himself to use those sullied words: freedom, brotherhood, or indeed even Germany? He gropes for them in the quiet sanctum which only the humble and believing dare approach. . . .
>
> Let us honor these priceless possessions for a while by silence, let us learn to do the right things for a while without speaking about them. A man who knows himself to be near death is resolute, but he is also silent. Without a word, indeed if he has to be misunderstood and solitary, he does what is needful and right and makes his sacrifice (GS III, 479–80).

This second turning point changed Bonhoeffer's way of life again. The verve of his existence turned back to his home and there the decisions of importance took place, no longer in church circles. How could he have stayed out and enjoyed the privileges of office while his brothers, sisters, and brothers-in-law risked their lives with their desperate political actions?

This time he even transformed his innermost commitments, such as his stand for Christian pacifism. Pursuing this would have endangered the much wider task of his family inside the conspiracy. Conscientious objection would have meant in this moment a rather private action or even an act of selfish faith.

All of this was bound to impose new marks on his theological scrutiny. The traces of these new marks, however, follow less coherently in Bonhoeffer's written work than those of the first mutation, but its furrows reach further and deeper. They found their preliminary fragmentary expression in *Letters and Papers from Prison* and have since then caught the imagination of many Christians as pointing to a new and valid concept of future Christian existence. They circle around the phrase of a "non-religious interpretation of the gospel in a world come of age," the term used almost exclusively by Bonhoeffer himself but picked up in the English-speaking world solely under the different and slightly shifting term of "religionless Christianity," which Bonhoeffer used only once.

Bonhoeffer must have felt that the witness of *The Cost of Discipleship* had lost some of its concrete features of protest and attack. Living it out suddenly appeared to keep one in a realm of respectable but irrelevant privacy and its structure appeared to be virtually an abstraction. The enthusiastically rediscovered church turned out to be sterile in its conception and liberal brothers and friends turned out to do the necessary Christian deeds. This situation had to be penetrated and theologically verbalized in a way that expressed the true character of

Christ and the true character of those worldly, secularized men. It was to serve *this* purpose that Bonhoeffer set out to rewrite his theology under the rubric of "non-religious interpretation of the gospel in a world come of age." The formulas he used certainly were no more than provisional labels in actual personal correspondence. But Bonhoeffer wanted in those terms to specify something to which, for the sake of the living Christ and his responsibly acting contemporaries, he attached great importance and which came to him as he put his theology to the test in his new situation. The twofold change of the direction of his way had made him realize how far traditional theologies and ecclesiastical structures had progressed on a track which lead to sterility; and here it is obvious that "man come of age" was not just the progressive happy optimist, becoming better and better, but the irreversibly grownup, autonomous adult who accepts his heavy responsibilities without escape into backward piety.

Certainly, "non-religious interpretation" opens up huge new problems for our theological conceptions. But we can already see that it aims at a protest against Christianity as a neatly separated and special realm of life. It also warns against a superficial and intellectual game of language or dogmatic definition. Obviously it is concerned with breaking away from social, legal, and political areas in which Christianity has happily settled down and prospered quite well for centuries. Certainly it must also be concerned with breaking down conceptual absolutes which have made either a tyrant out of or a much too expensive entrance ticket to faith. And centrally it aims at abandoning all that hopelessly betrays or dams up the message of the suffering, and by his powerlessness, conquering Jesus who is the witness of God's presence in this modern, wicked, and hopeful world.

If this is so, "non-religious interpretation" cannot be done overnight and self-identification with secular man cannot be reached by abandoning Christian identity. It cannot be done merely by means of a skillful exactitude of formulation, but only by a laborious combination of stringent theological thinking, concentrated prayer—because of our identity—and the daring action and reorganization that will spring from true penitence in the church. We will, then, experience the fact that "non-religious interpretation" is in no sense a negative dismissal of tradition—though one must be prepared to risk that. Nor is it a cheapening of all that Bonhoeffer was pointing toward as most costly in *The Cost of Discipleship*. Rather, it is an even more demanding exposition of all that is costly. *The Cost of Discipleship* had ended with a strong chapter on the *imitatio Christi; Letters and Papers from Prison* also finishes with a plea for the *imitatio* in its hints at "partaking in the sufferings of Christ in this world." But all this involves not an ideal of passive giving in, but rather the most active regaining of access to the sources of real life.

Of course, Bonhoeffer is not the only person who perceived such visions at that time and sealed them with his death. In strangely similar circumstances—incognito, misunderstanding, and ecclesiastical repudiation, and indeed in the same terrible year of 1944—and quite independently of one another, other witnesses expressed similar convictions: e.g., the Jewess Simone Weil and the French worker-priest, Henry Perrin. Their milieu was different, but what they deeply yearned for and what they foretold and represented was the same: the new image of Christian identity and Christian total identification with modern man in his forlornness, wickedness, responsibilities, and hopes.

In such people a new type of Christian martyr has entered into our time; no longer that saintly martyr, but the human and guilt-covered martyr; men who remain one of us and convince us of the compelling presence of the message; a type of Christian whose faith no longer places him in opposition to a wicked world in exemplary purity, but gives him mature solidarity with those who are entangled in inescapable responsibilities and can no longer withdraw into the lost circle of an untainted minority or of a happy tutelage under the competence of priests and pastors.

Here might be one of the keys for understanding Bonhoeffer's theological fragments, formulated after the second change in his life and including the whole witness given by the theologian, the Christian, and the contemporary.

To what we have tried to express here, Bonhoeffer himself gave finest expression in a letter he wrote the day after the plot of July 20 had failed. He was then convinced that the end of his personal and national hopes was close at hand. He calmly surveyed his past and present, pointing to the turning point of 1931 and to his position now, when all around him, including the official church, loudly condemned men like him:

"During the last year or so I have come to know and understand more and more the profound this-worldliness of Christianity. The Christian is not a homo religiosus, *but simply a man, as Jesus was a man. . . . I don't mean the shallow and banal this-worldliness of the enlightened, the busy, the comfortable, or the lascivious, but the profound this-worldliness, characterized by discipline and the constant knowledge of death and resurrection. . . .*

"I remember a conversation that I had in A[merica] thirteen years ago with a young French pastor. We were asking ourselves quite simply what we wanted to do with our lives. He said he would like to become a saint (and I think it is quite likely that he did become one). At that time I was very impressed but I disagreed with him, and said, in effect, that I should like to learn to have faith. For a long time I did not realize the depth of the contrast. I thought I could acquire faith by trying to live a holy life, or something like it. I suppose I wrote The Cost of Discipleship *as the end of that path. Today I can see the dangers of that book, though I still stand by what I wrote.*

"I discovered later, and I am still discovering right up to this moment, that it is only by living completely in this world that one learns to have faith. One must completely abandon any attempt to make something of oneself, whether it be a saint, or a converted sinner, or a churchman (a so-called priestly type!), a righteous man or an unrighteous one, a sick man or a healthy one. By this-worldliness I mean living unreservedly in life's duties, problems, successes and failures, experiences and perplexities. In so doing we throw ourselves completely into

*the arms of God, taking seriously, not our own suffer-
ings, but those of God in the world—watching with Christ
in Gethsemane. That, I think, is faith, that is* metanoia;
*and that is how one becomes a man and a Christian. . . .
How can success make us arrogant, or failure lead us
astray, when we share in God's sufferings through a life
of this kind?. . .*

"*I am glad to have been able to learn this, and I know
I have been able to do so only along the road that I have
travelled. So I am grateful for the past and present, and
content with them*" (LP 201–2).

THE OTHER LETTERS
FROM PRISON

by MARIA VON WEDEMEYER-WELLER

It would be presumptuous to think that I could add anything to the picture the theologian and man Dietrich Bonhoeffer that has been drawn so aptly and diligently by Eberhard Bethge in his recently published biography, *Dietrich Bonhoeffer* [Chr. Kaiser Verlag, 1967].[1] I write only because of my knowledge that our engagement was a source of strength to Dietrich. He was able to convert painful longing into gratitude for the fact that there was something to anticipate; he was able to convert self-reproach for the suffering he may have caused others into a joy that those relationships existed at all. Yes, he even had the ability to convert his annoyance at the limitations of our relationship, and the misunderstandings that resulted from them, into a hopeful and eager expectation and challenge. He was able to

[1] Anyone who knew Dietrich Bonhoeffer must be filled with admiration and gratitude to Bethge for his outstanding biography. No matter how well one may have known Dietrich Bonhoeffer, this work offers an abundance of new facts, insights, and explanations which could have been uncovered only by thorough and painstaking research throughout years of utter dedication. And no one but Bethge could have produced it. He is unique in his knowledge of Bonhoeffer, his background, and the thoughts with which he lived. Bethge has welded the three into a whole.

transform the fumblings and erratic emotions of a young girl into the assured certainty that this was an addition and a source of strength to his own life. These lines can be nothing more than the recollections of a girl, then nineteen years old, who very undeservedly had gained his love.

Early Life Together

My first encounter with Dietrich Bonhoeffer was in the home of my grandmother, Ruth von Kleist-Retzow. I was twelve years old and had asked to be included in the confirmation classes which Bonhoeffer conducted for my older brother and two cousins. The interview was held in the presence of my grandmother. I flunked. Whatever the reason may have been, I remember that it caused Dietrich considerable amusement and my grandmother none at all. Sunday church services were attended regularly by my grandmother at Finkenwalde, Dietrich's seminary. This involved lengthy commuting and was not always appreciated by her six grandchildren. We were, however, participants in many conversations with Dietrich that left us with little detailed information, but with an admiration and healthy respect for him. I remember one occasion when he told us about an exceptionally good sermon of one of his students, but voiced the criticism that the sermon was not recited from memory. He claimed that he had learned his first ten sermons by heart. At this point I quietly left the room for fear he might be tempted to prove his statement!

I saw him again after I graduated from high school and the rapport was immediate. Dietrich had the great gift of putting a person utterly at ease by accepting the level of the other with sincerity and commitment. We talked about mathematics. Neither of us knew much about the subject, but we managed to fill an evening with animated discussion of it. During the next fall I was in Berlin taking care of my grandmother, and Dietrich had ample opportunity to visit and talk. It amused him to take me to lunch at a small restaurant close to the hospital which was owned by Hitler's brother. He claimed there was no safer place to talk.

There was no urgency on his part, although he had great sensitivity to the changing levels of our friendship and to my willingness to receive his attention. When he wanted to present me to his family he had his niece, Renate Schleicher, later the wife of Eberhard Bethge, issue the invitation. It was a memorable evening of music-making and the only time I ever saw the entire family together. After our engagement Dietrich became less cautious. He had at first accepted a waiting period out of respect to my family, but soon he objected clearly, decisively, and repeatedly in letters and telephone calls to me. When we succeeded in changing the dictum, it was too late; he had been imprisoned.

Visiting the Prisoner

Our first meeting thereafter took place in the *Reichskriegsgericht* and I found myself being used as a tool by the prosecutor Roeder. I was brought into the room with practically no forewarning, and Dietrich was visibly shaken. He first reacted with silence, but then carried on a normal conversation; his emotions showed only in the pressure with which he held my hand. Thereafter I saw him fairly regularly, at least once a month. He was given permission to write a one-page letter every four days and alternated between his parents and me. There was no limitation on the number of letters I wrote other than the patience of the censor. Finally he found a friendly guard who smuggled letters in both directions. Most of Dietrich's letters to me are now in the Houghton Library at Harvard.[2] A few were lost in the hurried flight from the Russian invasion.

Dietrich often mentioned his reluctance to express his feelings. He pondered the differences between our two families and his own feelings of propriety and privacy. Yet when he felt the need to express them in a smuggled letter (or on those few times during my visits when the attending officer would tactfully leave the room), he did so with an intensity that surprised him more than it did me. When I decided to live with his parents in order to be closer, he wrote:

> It happens to be the case that certain things remain unsaid in my family, while they are expressed in yours. There is no point discussing what is the "right" way. It involves different people who act as they inwardly must. I can imagine that at first it will be hard for you that many things, especially in religious matters, remain unexpressed at home. But I would be very glad if you could succeed in adjusting to the ways of my parents as I have tried through your grandmother to adjust to the ways of your family. I have become increasingly grateful for this (undated).

[2] The Houghton Library has 38 letters (and other papers) which are not, however, accessible to the public. The following quotations are from these letters. Translation is the author's.—Ed.

From my visits I recall that his reaction to imprisonment took one of two forms, either confident hope that the end was clearly in sight, or utter annoyance at the fact that not enough pressure was applied to drive his case ahead. In connection with the latter he wrote: "How many 'scruples' (*Bedenklichkeiten*) repeatedly prevent our class from acting. I believe that the weakness of our class is based on its justified or unjustified scruples. Simple people are different. They make more mistakes, but they also do more good, because their road to action does not lead through scruple" (undated).

After one of my early visits he wrote:

You cannot imagine what it means in my present situation to have you. I am certain of God's special guidance here. The way in which we found each other and the time, so shortly before my imprisonment, are a clear sign for this. Again, it was a case of *hominum confusione et dei providentia*. Everyday I am overcome anew at how undeservedly I received this happiness, and each day I am deeply moved at what a hard school God has led you through during the last year. And now it appears to be his will that I have to bring you sorrow and suffering . . . so that our love for each other may achieve the right foundation and the right endurance. When I also think about the situation of the world, the complete darkness over our personal fate and my present imprisonment, then I believe that our union can only be a sign of God's grace and kindness, which calls us to faith. We would be blind if we did not see it. Jeremiah says at the moment of his people's great need "still one shall buy houses and acres in this land" as a sign of trust in the future. This is where faith belongs. May God give it to us daily. And I do not mean the faith which flees the world, but the one that endures the world and which loves and remains true to the world in spite of all the suffering which it contains for us. Our marriage shall be a yes to God's earth; it shall strengthen our courage to act and accomplish something on the earth. I fear that Christians who stand with only one leg upon earth also stand with only one leg in heaven (Aug. 12, 1943).

Dietrich encouraged me to plan the practical aspects of our future together. It helped him to envision a specific piece of furniture in our future apartment, a particular walk through the fields, a familiar spot on the beach. He never tired of urging me to learn better English or to resume practicing the violin, although both of these seemed irrelevant to me at the time. He was thoroughly and justifiably convinced that he was the better cook, but refused to think this important, or rather considered it just as unimportant as my interest in mathematics. But he enjoyed talking about details of our wedding; he had chosen the 103rd psalm as a text and claimed that he was working on the menu.

He advised me about what I should read and carefully indicated which of the books he had returned from prison were worth my reading. Yet he patiently read my favorites and commented on them with understanding. For example, he questioned my enthusiasm for Rilke. Discussing *Letters to a Young Poet* he wrote: "To me— and I trust also to you—Rilke would have written quite differently (though I am quite certain he would not have bothered to write to me at all). To make a musical comparison: I have to transpose Rilke continually from d-sharp major to c-major, and his pianissimo I would disregard at times—so would you" (Oct. 8, 1943).

I did make a dutiful attempt to read his books, starting from the beginning with *Sanctorum Communio*. When I admitted my frustration, it amused him thoroughly. He claimed that the only one of concern to him at that moment was *Life Together*, and he preferred that I wait until he was around to read it.

At least once a week we delivered books, laundry, and food, and picked up what he chose to return. It was important to Dietrich that he knew the day and time in advance, and because of air raids and disrupted transportation this was not always easy. He especially asked to be informed of a visit as far in advance as possible. "You cheat me out of the joy of anticipation," he would say, "and that is a very necessary part of your visit." There were some happy times during these visits. The fact that I brought a sizable Christmas tree all the way from home created great hilarity with both the guards and Dietrich. He remarked that maybe if he moved his cot out of his cell and stood up for the Christmas season he could accommodate the tree comfortably. It ended up in the guards' room where Dietrich was invited to enjoy it. He teased me about it often and complained that I had not brought an Easter bunny for Easter. But he also wrote: "Isn't it so that even when we are laughing, we are a bit sad."

Life in Prison

He lived by church holidays and by seasons, rather than by the calendar month, and the dates on his letters were sometimes approximations at best. He voiced his disappointment that he had not received a letter from me or anyone else expressly for Whitsunday. About Advent he wrote: "A prison cell, in which one waits, hopes, does various unessential things, and is completely dependent on the fact that the door of freedom has to be opened *from the outside,* is not a bad picture of Advent" (Nov. 21, 1943).

Once, during the summer, he was permitted to sit in the prison yard while writing a letter to me:

> The sun is a special favorite of mine and has reminded me often of the fact that man is created from earth and does not consist of air and thoughts. This went so far that once, when I was asked to preach in Cuba at Christmas time, coming from the ice of North America into the blooming vegetation, I almost succumbed to the sun cult and hardly knew what I should have preached. It was a real crisis, and something of this comes over me every summer when I feel the sun. To me the sun is not an astronomical entity, but something like a living power which I love and fear. I find it cowardly to look past these realities rationally. . . . So must patience, joy, gratitude and calm assert themselves against all sorts of resistance. It says in the psalm "God is sun and shield." To recognize and experience and believe this is a moment of great grace and by no means an everyday wisdom (Aug. 20, 1943).

He looked forward to being included in the life that was led at my home. We made a bet about whether I would be able to teach him to dance: he thought that I could, while I considered him a hopeless case. It would have been a private exercise anyway, because he did not think that a minister should dance in public. He also wanted to learn horseback riding, yet hunting was not to his taste. "Did you know that Friedrich Wilhelm the

First would ask any minister he met if hunting was a sin—he was a passionate hunter—and I think all of them, including A. H. Franke, were reasonable enough to declare that it was not. Yet it is, like many other things, not everyone's business" (Nov. 21, 1943).

He also looked forward to big family events, albeit with a certain reluctance:

You can hardly imagine how I long for everyone: after these long months of solitude. I have a real hunger for people. I am afraid, however, that at first I shall have trouble enduring long gatherings of many people. Even in times past I could endure family festivities, which in fact I love dearly, only if I could escape into my room for half an hour from time to time. From now on I hope you will escape with me. Yet you must not think me unsociable. Unfortunately, I find people extremely exhausting. But of these social vices and virtues you will learn soon enough (Dec. 1, 1943).

As time went on there were, of course, moments of discouragement:

It would be better if I succeeded in writing to you only of my gratitude, my joy, and my happiness in having you and in keeping the pressure and the impatience of this long imprisonment out of sight. But that would not be truthful, and it would appear to me as an injustice to you. You must know how I really feel and must not take me for a pillar saint (*Saeulenheiligen*) . . . I can't very well imagine that you would want to marry one in the first place—and I would also advise against it from my knowledge of church history (Aug. 20, 1943).

Slowly it gets to be a waiting whose outward sense I cannot comprehend; the inward reason must be found daily. Both of us have lost infinitely much during the past months; time today is a costly commodity, for who knows how much more time is given to us. And yet I do not dare to think that it was or is lost time either for each of us individually or for both of us together. We have grown together in a different way than we have thought and wished, but these are unusual times and will remain so a while longer, and everything depends on our being one in the essential things and on our remaining with each other. Your life would have been quite different, easier, clearer, simpler had not our path crossed a year ago. But there are only short moments when this thought bothers me. I believe that not only I, but you too, had arrived at the moment in life when we had to meet, neither of us basically has any desire for an easy life, much as we may enjoy beautiful and happy hours in this life, and much as we may have a great longing for these hours today. I believe that happiness lies for both of us at a different and hidden place which is incomprehensible to many. Actually both of us look for challenges (*Aufgaben*), up to now each for himself, but from now on together. Only in this work will we grow completely together when God gives us the time for it (Sept. 20, 1943).

Stifter once said "pain is a holy angel, who shows treasures to men which otherwise remain forever hidden; through him men have become greater than through all joys of the world." It must be so and I tell this to myself in my present position over and over again—the pain of longing which often can be felt even physically, must be there, and we shall not and need not talk it away. But it needs to be overcome every time, and thus there is an even holier angel than the one of pain, that is the one of joy in God (Nov. 21, 1943).

The Last Letter

Dietrich was moved to the Gestapo prison in October, 1944. It was then impossible to obtain visitation permits, and it is improbable that any of my letters reached him there. When the prison was badly damaged during an air raid in February he was moved out of Berlin and my attempts to find him in either Dachau, Buchenwald, or Flossenbürg failed. In his last letter to me on Christmas, 1944, he wrote:

These will be quiet days in our homes. But I have had the experience over and over again that the quieter it is around me, the clearer do I feel the connection to you. It is as though in solitude the soul develops senses which we hardly know in everyday life. Therefore I have not felt lonely or abandoned for one moment. You, the parents, all of you, the friends and students of mine at the front, all are constantly present to me. Your prayers and good thoughts, words from the Bible, discussions long past, pieces of music, and books,—[all these] gain life and reality as never before. It is a great invisible sphere in which one lives and in whose reality there is no doubt. If it says in the old children's song about the angels: "Two, to cover me, two, to wake me," so is this guardianship (*Bewahrung*), by good invisible powers in the morning and at night, something which grownups need today no less than children. Therefore you must not think that I am unhappy. What is happiness and unhappiness? It depends so little on the circumstances; it depends really only on that which happens inside a person. I am grateful every day that I have you, and that makes me happy (Dec. 19, 1944).

READING BONHOEFFER IN ENGLISH TRANSLATION: SOME DIFFICULTIES

by JOHN D. GODSEY

My intention in what follows is to locate and discuss
some of the difficulties I have observed in the translation
of Dietrich Bonhoeffer's writings into the English language. I have no interest in casting aspersions on translators, editors, or publishers on either side of the Atlantic,
to all of whom the English-speaking public owes an
immense debt of gratitude. Rather, I wish merely to aid
the unsuspecting reader who has no access to the original
German by pinpointing problems arising from specific
editorial or translational decisions. The thoroughness of
my investigation of particular books has varied, so that
in some cases I shall limit myself to general comments
or a few specific observations. In others, especially *Letters and Papers from Prison,* my analysis will be more
detailed.

Confusing Titles

Let us begin by examining the titles of Bonhoeffer's
books. I have never been able to understand why British
and American publishers could not agree on a common
title for the same book. In our day of technological advance the English-speaking communities are so closely
linked that the practice of having differing titles can

only result in confusion. To preclude any misunderstanding, readers are hereby informed that identical texts are to be found under these different titles: *Sanctorum Communio* (British) and *The Communion of Saints* (American), *Christology* (British) and *Christ the Center* (American), *Letters and Papers from Prison* (British and American) and *Prisoner for God* (American). In the first two instances the British publishers have rendered literally the German title and in the latter have selected the subtitle of the German edition, the full translation of which is *Resistance and Submission: Letters and Papers from Prison.*

The Proliferation of Editions

The problem of quoting Bonhoeffer in English has become a nightmare, not simply because of the confusing titles, which would be bad enough, but because of the ever growing number of editions. The introduction of the cheaper paperbacks has caused the greatest havoc, because in almost every case it has meant a different pagination. This is true, for instance, of *Letters and Papers from Prison, Ethics, The Cost of Discipleship, Creation and Fall,* and *Temptation* (the latter two have now been combined in one paperback). Nevertheless, other factors are sometimes involved, and to these we now turn.

The Cost of Discipleship, the first of Bonhoeffer's books available in English, appeared in 1948 as an abridged translation that omitted five sections of the original. This was followed in 1959 by a second hardback edition that included the omitted sections and made minor revisions in the translation. This revised and unabridged text has been used in the paperback edition, which means there are now three editions of this book with three different paginations!

The story has been quite different with *Ethics*. A complete translation of the first German edition appeared in hardback in 1955. In the sixth German edition of 1963, Eberhard Bethge, the editor of these posthumously published fragments, changed the order of the various chapters to conform with what he believes to be their proper chronology and added a new foreword to explain the reasons for the changes. In 1965 the paperback edition that appeared in English followed this improved arrangement but then failed to include a translation of Bethge's valuable foreword.

When it comes to problems of quotation, *Letters and Papers from Prison* is in a class by itself! By placing new materials in an appendix, the basic German text has been kept the same through twelve editions. In contrast, the English editions not only appear under different titles, as mentioned above, but also in four differing paginations! First of all, there is the original hardback edition of 1953, entitled *Letters and Papers from Prison* in Great Britain and *Prisoner for God* in America. From this basic translation have come two paperback editions, both called *Letters and Papers from Prison*. The American edition is a Macmillan paperback, whereas the British edition is published in Collins' Fontana Book series. In the latter the arrangement of the text is altered, Bonhoeffer's poems being taken from their normal positions and placed together at the end of the book. A second hardback edition was published in Britain (never in America!) in 1956; this contained no revision of the translation but added in an appendix Bonhoeffer's "Report on Prison Life" and Bethge's account of "The Last Days," as well as an Index of Names and Subjects. Finally, a third edition, revised and enlarged, has appeared in Great Britain in 1967 and is being published in both hardback and paperback editions in America. This vastly improved edition will be discussed in detail later.

Some Miscellaneous Problems

Every serious student of Bonhoeffer probably has a list of things he has noticed "along the way," as it were—incidental observations about translations, omissions, mistakes, and so forth. I now want to share some of the items on my list before moving on to more serious analysis.

(1) First, a word of genuine appreciation is due the translators of Bonhoeffer's two earliest works, *Sanctorum Communio* (*The Communion of Saints*) and *Act and Being*. These tersely written, highly complicated dissertations have been rendered into English with unusual care and felicity, and only those who have read the German can fully appreciate this accomplishment. Many readers may be unaware that the English text of *Sanctorum Communio* incorporates substantial sections of Bonhoeffer's dissertation which had been removed at the time of original publication and thus is superior even to the latest German edition, which prints the additions in an appendix.

(2) *Christ the Center* is the title chosen for the American edition of Bethge's reconstruction from students' notes of Bonhoeffer's lectures on Christology at the University of Berlin in 1933. I question whether this title represents the central thrust of these lectures. Would not "The Present Christ" have been more appropriate? Whereas a detailed analysis of this translation would be interesting, considerations of space require me to limit my comments to one item. This concerns the omission at the top of page 177 of one whole sentence present in the original German and of an important word in the succeeding sentence. The text should read as follows:

Is it [the empty tomb] the decisive fact of christology? Was it really empty? Is it the visible attestation, the lifting of the incognito? Is Jesus' divine Sonship made public to everyone, and is faith superfluous? If it was not empty, then is Christ not risen and our faith vain?

(3) Whether it came about because of the original abridgement of the text or because it was considered to be more logical or helpful, the division of the English version of *The Cost of Discipleship* (the German title is simply *Nachfolge*, i.e., *Discipleship*) into four distinct chapters makes it extremely difficult to discover Bonhoeffer's strategy in this book. He himself divided the work into two parts, the first being an exposition of discipleship as found in the Synoptic Gospels, the second showing how this understanding of the relationship between the disciples and their Lord is translated into the churchly terminology of the Apostle Paul. Lutheran theologians have characteristically begun with Pauline

theology and have tended to exalt the Pauline Christ above the Christ of the Gospels. Bonhoeffer, a Lutheran, deliberately began with the Gospels with the intention of demonstrating that the Christ who is present in the church for us today is as much the Jesus of the Synoptists as the Christ of Paul. He is convinced that the difference in terminology involves no rupture in the unity of the Scriptural witness. In order to make Bonhoeffer's intention clear, the Table of Contents as he arranged it for the German edition is reproduced below and can be compared with the English:

CONTENTS

Matthew 6: Of the Hidden Character of the
Christian Life
The Hidden Righteousness
The Hiddenness of Prayer
The Hiddenness of the Devout Life
The Simplicity of the Carefree Life
Matthew 7: The Separation of the Disciple
Community
The Disciples and the Unbelievers
The Great Divide
The Conclusion
The Messengers (Exposition of Matthew 10)

II.

The Church of Jesus Christ and Discipleship—
Preliminary Questions
Baptism
The Body of Christ
The Visible Community
The Saints
The Image of Christ

(4) Some people have complained that the translation
of *Life Together* is a bit too "sweet," by which they pre-
sumably mean that the English fails to convey the
strength and masculinity of Bonhoeffer's German style.
This is probably correct, but it is also true that the translator has aided the English-speaking reader by providing
frequent subheadings in each chapter. My chief regret

regarding this book is the omission of the author's brief foreword, which clearly sets forth his aim. Its inclusion would have precluded the false impression which some people have received that Bonhoeffer was describing the *only true pattern* of Christian living rather than merely a remarkable experiment. The foreword reads as follows (my translation):

> An essential characteristic of the subject treated here is that it can be furthered only through joint effort. Because it concerns, not an affair of private groups, but rather a task given to the church, it is likewise not a matter of more or less accidental, individual solutions, but of a common responsibility of the church. The understandable reticence in the handling of this task, which has hardly begun to be grasped, must gradually give way to a readiness in the church to lend assistance. The multiplicity of new forms of community within the church necessitates the watchful cooperation of all responsible people. The following study should not be considered as more than just one contribution to the comprehensive question and possibly also as an aid toward clarification and practice.

(5) For years Eberhard Bethge has been trying to correct his own error in regard to when *Temptation* was written. These Bible studies, which have been called the most "Lutheran" of all Bonhoeffer's works, were presented at the reunion of his Finkenwalde students during the latter part of June, 1938. The "Note" at the beginning of the book, which publishers seem unwilling to modify, should be changed accordingly.

(6) Two of the projected three volumes of an English edition of Bonhoeffer's "Collected Works" have appeared under the titles *No Rusty Swords* and *The Way to Free-*

dom. While appreciative of having more of Bonhoeffer's writings in English and without overlooking the time and effort involved in such an undertaking, I must confess my disappointment in the result. In the first place, who would ever guess from the titles that these were "Collected Works"? Secondly, instead of a factual table of contents which would make it possible to find a particular writing, one is confronted with an almost useless biographical-chronological construction of the editor. Thirdly, economic considerations have apparently overridden the interests of scholarship, so that instead of a creative attempt to improve Bethge's meticulously edited four volumes of *Gesammelte Schriften* by reproducing the whole in English *in strictly chronological order*, we are left with an arbitrary selection loosely tied together by a running commentary that leaves much to be desired. Finally, in my opinion the space consumed by the editor's Introductions would have been better used to present more of Bonhoeffer himself, and I draw some comfort from the fact that the "Imaginary Conversation" between Bonhoeffer and H. Richard Niebuhr has been excised from the American edition of *The Way to Freedom.*

(7) Varying translations of the same German word or phrase are always of interest, and I wish to call attention to a few of these. A key word in Bonhoeffer's Christology as well as in his understanding of Christian living is *Stellvertretung,* which can mean either (or both) taking another's place or acting in another's behalf. In *Sanctorum Communio* the word is usually translated "vicarious action," in *Ethics* "deputyship," and elsewhere often

"representation." In his earliest works Bonhoeffer often calls the church *"Christus als Gemeinde existierend,"* which is sometimes translated "Christ existing as community," sometimes "Christ existing as the church." In the latter instance it is important to remember that he does not mean the church as institution, but as a communion of persons. In *Ethics* and *Letters and Papers from Prison* Bonhoeffer speaks of marriage, labor, government (or state), and church as divine *"Mandaten."* In the former book the word is translated "mandates," in the latter (first edition) "decrees." "Mandate" better expresses Bonhoeffer's meaning of imposed task or concrete commission. My concluding observation (this could go on and on!) has to do with the meaning of *"mündig"* in the well-known phrase found in the prison letters, *"die mündige Welt."* This phrase is variously translated "The world come of age," "the mature world," and "the adult world." It is important to remember that the word *"mündig"* in German refers to that time when a young person turns twenty-one and not to the adult maturity of the wise old sage!

The Translation of Letters and Papers from Prison

The recently published Revised and Enlarged Edition of *Letters and Papers from Prison* (SCM Press and The Macmillan Company, 1967) is so superior that, in my judgment, all copies of previous editions should be gathered together and burned. Since the English-language editions account for the majority of the more than 300,000 copies that have been sold in translation, this would produce quite a bonfire!

My enthusiastic endorsement of the new edition rests primarily on the improved style and accuracy of the translation, but before demonstrating this I would like to call attention to a number of added features which alone would warrant accolades. At the beginning is a sermon entitled "The Saint of the Secular," preached by Dr. J. A. T. Robinson at the Dietrich Bonhoeffer Memorial Church in London on the occasion of the twentieth anniversary of Bonhoeffer's death. Because of the "Honest to God" controversy, some might consider the inclusion of a sermon by the Bishop of Woolwich a mixed blessing, but I find his words a sensitive and moving tribute. Next, there is a new foreword by the editor, Eberhard Bethge, in which he contrasts the reception of Bonhoeffer's last fragmentary writings in the German-speaking and English-speaking areas during the past fifteen years and proposes the thesis that what makes Bonhoeffer so attractive is the way he holds in unity three elements—theology, ecclesiology, and ethics. Further, there is the addition of seven photographs, three poems ("The Friend," "Jonah," and "The Past"), Bonhoeffer's "Report on Prison Life," Bethge's account of "The Last Days," a General Index with 269 entries, and a revised and enlarged Index of Biblical References (throughout the text many biblical references are for the first time identified and others are corrected). Finally, two new letters are added (Oct. 22, 1943 and Feb. 4, 1944) and two letters properly identified (Nov. 30, 1943, which was earlier included as a part of the letter of Nov. 29, and Aug. 14, 1944, earlier a part of the letter of Aug. 10.).

The meticulous care exercised in the revision of the text in accordance with the twelfth German edition is attested by the many small, but sometimes very important, improvements that are noticeable throughout. Not only are the dates of letters corrected (July 25 instead of July 27, 1943; Dec. 25 instead of Dec. 31, 1943; March 2 instead of March 3, 1944) and dates assigned to Bonhoeffer's "Wedding Sermon" (May, 1943) and his "Thoughts on the Baptism of D. W. R." (May, 1944), but also in almost all cases the English now follows the German much more faithfully in indicating by ellipses (. . .) the breaks in the text (those parts of letters that Bethge chose to omit), in inserting Bonhoeffer's quotation marks, and in italicizing the words he wished to emphasize. Footnotes are greatly multiplied, names which heretofore were indicated only by initials are now given in full, and quotations from German literary works are left in the original language, literal translations being provided in footnotes.

Every translator worth his salt takes certain liberties with the text he is trying to render into the idiom of another language—a small omission here, a reasonable paraphrase there, and so on. Usually these go unnoticed and are relatively unimportant, anyway. I am sure that the original translator of Bonhoeffer's *Letters and Papers from Prison* never dreamed they would come to assume such an important place in the thought of Christians (and non-Christians!) during the second half of the twentieth century. As luck would have it, people now have a vital interest in every word Bonhoeffer wrote. A revision of the translation became inevitable, and in the process a number of sins of omission and commission have, to use a colloquial expression, "come home to roost."

A careful comparison of the original and the revised translations, and of both with the German text, discloses, first of all, that the revision is distinguished by an improved style. Words flow more smoothly, and sentences more accurately reflect the syntax and rhythm of the German. Beyond the stylistic improvement, however, one discovers that the revised translation is remarkably more accurate and faithful to the German text. Literally dozens of omissions (words, phrases, clauses, sentences, and even a whole paragraph!) and significant variations are evident, and several mistranslations. Admittedly, the great majority of these are of slight importance for the overall interpretation of Bonhoeffer's thought; nevertheless, the cumulative effect is impressive, and in a few instances decisive differences come to light. Within the limits of this article I can of course present only a few examples of omissions, variants, and mistranslations, and to illustrate the problem of the proliferation of editions as well as to aid as many as possible in locating quotations or omissions, I shall always indicate four page numbers in this order: (1) The newly revised English hardback edition (which will usually be quoted in the case of omissions); (2) the first English hardback edition; (3) the first English paperback edition (Macmillan); (4) the twelfth German edition.

We will begin by pointing out some rather trivial but interesting differences in the translation of certain words that reappear throughout the book. In the revised translation "Father" and "Mother" are used instead of "Papa" and "Mama" when Bonhoeffer addresses his parents (here the original translation is correct!); *Revier* is rightly translated "sick bay" rather than "guardroom"; *Methodismus* is rendered "methodism" instead of "asceticism"; the well-known German word "*Losungen*" is left to designate the "daily texts" that the Moravians have published annually since 1731; "baptism" consistently replaces "christening"; and "pagans" is preferred to "heathen" or "unbelievers."

Relatively unimportant omissions are found in these sentences: "That is why I value Stifter and Gotthelf so much" (107, 82, 108, 118) and "I would include the Magdeburg virgins and the Naumburg sculptures" (145, 115, 153, 167). The missing parts of the two sentences are, respectively, "and Gotthelf" and "and the Naumburg sculptures." To illustrate the omission of a multitude of entire sentences, I shall choose two examples from "After Ten Years." At the conclusion of "Who stands fast?" Bonhoeffer asks, "Where are these responsible people?" (28, 16, 19, 13). In the middle of the section on "Confidence" he says, "We now know that only such confidence, which is always a venture, though a glad and positive venture, enables us really to live and work" (34f., 22, 27, 23). By the way, if one really wants to have fun, I suggest he compare the original and revised translations of "After Ten Years" with the rendering of the same passage in the Chime paperback entitled "I Loved This People"! The latter is actually more accurate in some cases; for instance, "*Dummheit*" is called "stupidity" rather than "folly."

Turning to more significant omissions, we find Bonhoeffer, in speaking of "the feeling of time," saying: "Our past is always kept before us by thankfulness and penitence" (88, 65, 85, 93). Concerning resistance and submission (*Widerstand und Ergebung*), he declares that "both of them must exist, and both must be practised" (134, 104, 138, 151). After expressing his opinion that the only times he had really changed was when he was first abroad and when he was under the first conscious influence of his father's personality, Bonhoeffer confesses, "It was then that I turned from phraseology to reality" (149, 119, 159, 174). Bonhoeffer characterizes the new language the church will someday speak as "perhaps quite non-religious, but liberating and redeeming—as was Jesus' language" (172, 140, 188, 207). When he tells us that we must live in the world *etsi deus non daretur,* he asserts that "God himself compels us to recognize it" (196, 163, 219, 241). The final case of omission I will mention here is the one I consider to be the most egregious of all, and it remains inexplicably unremedied in the revised translation! I have in mind a very important line that is omitted in the poem, "Who Am I?" I shall locate it by placing my translation of the missing line between the one that precedes it and the one that follows:

> thirsting for words of kindness, for neighbourliness,
> trembling with anger over arbitrary treatment and humiliation of the pettiest sort,
> tossing in expectation of great events, (197, 165, 221, 243).

We close with some examples of mistranslation: "those three were closest to me," not "these three were my most

promising pupils" (63, 48, 63, 61); "that the duty had
been laid on me to hold out in this boundary situation
with all its problems," not "that it was my duty to face
the worst" (87, 64, 85, 92); "I hope you don't think I
am here turning out to be a 'man of the inner line'" (a
churchman who disliked Hitler's anti-Christian dictator-
ship, but who, under pressure, abandoned his opposition
to it), not "I hope you don't think I am going to pieces
here" (90, 66, 88, 96); "You needn't worry—it will *not* be a
roman à clef" (a type of novel which depicts an actual
situation, but in which all the characters are dis-
guised), not "You needn't worry, it won't be a best-
seller!" (123, 97, 128, 140); "I should consider it a complete mistake . . . to proceed on 'methodist' lines here,"
not "I thought it would be a mistake . . . to be too rigid
about it" (132, 103, 137, 149); "who Christ really is, for
us today," not "what *is* Christ, for us to-day?" (152, 122,
162, 178); "exploiting human weakness or human boundaries," not "helping out human weakness or on the bor-
ders of human existence" (154, 124, 165, 181); "the
transcendence of epistemological theory has nothing to
do with the transcendence of God," not "the transcendence of theory based on perception has nothing to do
with the transcendence of God" (155, 124, 166, 182).

Further: "in the dispute between the Church and the
world," not "in the dispute between Christ and the
world" (180, 147, 197, 218); "though in his case [Paul]
the encounter with Jesus preceded the realization of sin,"
not "though in his case the knowledge of sin preceded
his encounter with Jesus" (189, 157, 209, 231); "the
secrets known to a man's valet . . . have become

the hunting-ground of modern pastoral workers," not "the secrets known by a man's valet . . . have become the hunting ground of modern psychotherapists" (191, 158, 212, 233); "in the one case it is social, financial, or political blackmail, and in the other, religious blackmail," not "they practise social, financial and political blackmail on their victims: the psychotherapists practise religious blackmail" (191, 158, 212, 234); "To be a Christian does not mean to be religious in a particular way, to make something of oneself (a sinner, a penitent, or a saint) on the basis of some method or other, but to be a man— not a type of man, but the man that Christ creates in us," not "To be a Christian does not mean to be religious in a particular way, to cultivate some particular form of asceticism (as a sinner, a penitent or a saint), but to be a man" (198, 166, 222f., 244).

Finally: "(b) the religionlessness of man who has come of age," not "(b) the decay of religion in a world that has come of age" (209, 178, 236, 258); "(b) Who is God?" not "(b) What do we mean by 'God'?" (209, 179, 237, 259); "His [Jesus'] 'being there for others' is the experience of transcendence," not "This concern of Jesus for others the experience of transcendence" (209, 179, 237, 259); "our relation to God is a new life in 'existence for others,' through participation in the being of Jesus," not "Our relation to God . . . [is] a new life for others, through participation in the Being of God" (210, 179, 238, 260); "The transcendental is not infinite and unattainable tasks, but the neighbor who is within reach in any situation," not "The transcendence consists not in tasks beyond our scope and power, but in the nearest thing to hand" (210, 179, 238, 260); "oriental religions," not "other religions" (210, 179, 238, 260).

Disagreeing with both translations in one instance, I want to propose the following: "The church is the church only when it is there for others" (cf. 211, 180, 239, 261). This maintains Bonhoeffer's intended parallelism with his view of Jesus as the man who is "there for others." Also, it should be pointed out that the revised translation is not without error. For example, the concluding sentence in the poem "Jonah" is completely misleading. Rather than "The sea was there," it should be translated "Then the sea was still" (223). The meaning is that when the guilty Jonah was thrown overboard, the sea ceased its raging and became calm.

I am aware that this report has been very detailed and condensed, but I think those who are familiar with Bonhoeffer's work will be able to recognize the context and the importance of some of the changes in translation. Others will have to do their homework! In working through this material one thing has impressed itself upon me with increasing force, namely, the heavy responsibility that must be assumed by those engaged in projects of translation.

BIBLIOGRAPHY

Prepared by PETER VORKINK, II

The following bibliography contains books and articles published in English by or about Dietrich Bonhoeffer through the spring of 1967.

Works by Bonhoeffer

Act and Being. Translated by Bernard Noble with an introduction by Ernst Wolf. New York: Harper & Row, 1962.

Christ the Center. Translated by John Bowden with an introduction by Edwin H. Robertson. New York: Harper & Row, 1966. British edition entitled *Christology.* London: William Collins Sons, 1966.

The Communion of Saints. Translated by Ronald Gregor Smith and others. New York: Harper & Row, 1963. British edition entitled *Sanctorum Communio.* London: William Collins Sons, 1963.

"Concerning the Christian Idea of God," *The Journal of Religion,* XII (April, 1932), 177–85.

The Cost of Discipleship. Translated by Reginald H. Fuller with memoir by G. Leibholz. New York: Macmillan, 1st ed., abridged, 1948; 2d ed., unabridged and revised, 1959; paperback edition, 1963.

Creation and Fall. Translated by John C. Fletcher. New York: Macmillan, 1959; paperback edition, 1965.

Ethics. Edited by Eberhard Bethge. Translated by Neville Horton Smith. New York: Macmillan, 1955; paperback edition (based on 6th German edition), 1963.

Gesammelte Schriften. Edited by Eberhard Bethge. 4 vols. München: Chr. Kaiser Verlag, 1958–1961. (Contains several selections in English.)

I Loved This People. Translated by Keith R. Crim with an introduction by Hans Rothfels. Richmond: John Knox Press, 1965.

Letters and Papers from Prison. Edited by Eberhard Bethge. Translated by Reginald H. Fuller. London: SCM Press, 1st ed., 1953; 2d ed. revised, 1956. American edition entitled *Prisoner for God*. New York: Macmillan, 1954; paperback edition entitled *Letters and Papers from Prison*, 1962; 3d ed. revised and enlarged, New York: Macmillan, 1967.

Life Together. Translated with an introduction by John W. Doberstein. New York: Harper & Row, 1954.

No Rusty Swords: Letters, Lectures and Notes 1928–1936 from the Collected Works of Dietrich Bonhoeffer Volume I. Translated by Edwin H. Robertson and John Bowden. Edited with an introduction by Edwin H. Robertson. New York: Harper & Row, 1965.

Preface to Bonhoeffer: The Man and Two of His Shorter Writings. Translated with an introduction by John D. Godsey. Philadelphia: Fortress Press, 1965.

Temptation. Translated by Kathleen Downham. New York: Macmillan, 1955; paperback edition, 1965.

The Way to Freedom: Letters, Lectures and Notes 1935–1939 from the Collected Works of Dietrich Bonhoeffer Volume II. Translated by Edwin H. Robertson and John Bowden. Edited with an introduction by Edwin H. Robertson. New York: Harper & Row, 1967.

Works about Bonhoeffer

EXTENDED TREATMENTS

BETHGE, EBERHARD. "The Challenge of Dietrich Bonhoeffer's Life and Theology," *The Chicago Theological Seminary Register*, LI (February, 1961), 1–38.

————. *Dietrich Bonhoeffer*. München: Chr. Kaiser Verlag., 1967. (English translation in preparation)

GODSEY, JOHN D. *The Theology of Dietrich Bonhoeffer*. Philadelphia: Westminster Press, 1960.

GOULD, WILLIAM BLAIR. *The Worldly Christian: Bonhoeffer on Discipleship*. Philadelphia: Fortress Press, 1967.

MARTY, MARTIN E. (ed.). *The Place of Bonhoeffer*. New York: Association Press, 1962.

PHILLIPS, JOHN A. *Christ for Us in the Theology of Dietrich Bonhoeffer*. New York: Harper & Row, 1967.

ROBERTSON, E. H. *Dietrich Bonhoeffer*. "Makers of Contemporary Theology." Richmond: John Knox Press, 1966.

SMITH, RONALD GREGOR (ed.). *World Come of Age*. Introduction by R. G. Smith. Philadelphia: Fortress Press, 1967.

ZIMMERMANN, W. D. and SMITH, RONALD GREGOR (eds.). *I Knew Dietrich Bonhoeffer*. Introduction by W. A. Visser 't Hooft. New York: Harper & Row, 1967.

ARTICLES, ESSAYS, AND RELATED WORKS

BARTLEY, W. W. "The Bonhoeffer Revival," *The New York Review of Books*, August 26, 1965.

BELL, G. K. A. *The Church and Humanity, 1939–1946*. London: Longmans, Green & Co., 1946. Chapters 18 & 20.

————. "The Church and the Resistance Movement in Germany," *The Wiener Library Bulletin*, XI, Nos. 3–4, pp. 21–23.

————. "Letters from a Nazi Prison," *Time and Tide*, XXXIV (1953), 1216.

BERGER, PETER L. "Camus, Bonhoeffer and the World Come of Age," *The Christian Century*, LXXVI (April 8 & 15, 1959), 417–18, 450–52.

BETHGE, EBERHARD. "Dietrich Bonhoeffer," *The Student Movement*, LVI, No. 3 (1954), 24–26. The same article appeared in *Campus Lutheran*, VI (December, 1954), 20–23.

————. "Dietrich Bonhoeffer," in *German Life and Letters*. Oxford: Basil Blackwell, 1957. Pp. 126–30. The same article appeared in *World Dominion*, XXXV (April, 1957), 77–81.

—————. "Dietrich Bonhoeffer: An Account of His Life," *The Plough*, III, No. 2 (1955), 35–42.

—————. "The Editing and Publishing of the Bonhoeffer Papers," *The Andover Newton Bulletin*, LII (December, 1959), 1–24.

BOROWITZ, E. B. "Bonhoeffer's World Come of Age," *Judaism*, XIV (Winter, 1965), 81–87.

BUSING, PAUL F. W. "Reminiscences of Finkenwalde," *The Christian Century*, LXXVIII (September 20, 1961), 1108–1111.

COX, HARVEY. "Beyond Bonhoeffer," *Commonweal*, LXXXII (September 17, 1965), 653–57.

—————. "Using and Misusing Bonhoeffer," *Christianity and Crisis*, XXIV (October 19, 1964), 199–201.

DE JONG, PIETER. "Camus and Bonhoeffer on the Fall," *Canadian Journal of Theology*, VII (October, 1961), 245–57.

DOWNING, F. GERALD. "Man's Coming of Age: Dietrich Bonhoeffer and Christianity Without Religion," *Prism*, No. 68 (December, 1962).

DUDZUS, D. "Discipleship and Worldliness in the Thinking of Dietrich Bonhoeffer," *Religion in Life*, XXXV (Spring, 1966), 230–40.

EBELING, GERHARD. "The Non-religious Interpretation of Biblical Concepts," and "Dietrich Bonhoeffer," in *Word and Faith*. Philadelphia: Fortress Press, 1963.

EBERSOLE, MARC C. *Christian Faith and Man's Religion*. New York: Thomas Y. Crowell Co., 1961. Chapter 3, "The Christian Faith without Religion."

ELSON, J. T. "Man for Others," *Life*, LVIII (May 7, 1965), 108–9.

FACKENHEIM, EMIL L. "On the Self-Exposure of Faith to the Modern Secular World: Philosophical Reflections in Light of Jewish Experience," *Daedalus*, XCVI, No. 1, pp. 193–219.

FENNELL, WILLIAM O. "Dietrich Bonhoeffer: The Man of Faith in a World Come of Age," *Canadian Journal of Theology*, VIII (1962), 172–80.

GILMOUR, S. M. "Seven on Bonhoeffer," *The Christian Century*, LXXIX (October 17, 1962), 1260.

GODSEY, JOHN D. "Theology from a Prison Cell," *The Drew Gateway*, XXVII (Spring, 1957), 139–54.

———. "Barth and Bonhoeffer," *The Drew Gateway*, XXXIII (Autumn, 1962), 3–20.

GREEN, CLIFFORD. "Bonhoeffer's Concept of Religion," *Union Seminary Quarterly Review*, XIX (November, 1963), 11–21.

GUALTIERI, A. R. "Dietrich Bonhoeffer's Ethics; Law, Freedom and Responsible Action," *Encounter*, XXVI (Summer, 1965), 349–61.

HARDWICK, E. "The Place of Bonhoeffer," *Heythrop Journal*, V (July, 1964), 297–99.

HAMILTON, WILLIAM. "A Secular Theology for a World Come of Age," *Theology Today*, XVIII (January, 1962), 435–59.

———. "Bonhoeffer: Christology and Ethic United," *Christianity and Crisis*, XXIV (October 19, 1964), 195–99.

———. "Faith and the Facts of Life," *The Nation*, CC (April 19, 1965), 424–26.

———. *The New Essence of Christianity*. New York: Association Press, 1961.

HEERING, H. J. "Meaning of Authority and Autonomy for Modern Man," *Congregational Quarterly*, XXXIV (January, 1956), 20–27.

HILL, GEORGE G. "Bonhoeffer, Bridge between Liberalism and Orthodoxy," *Christian Advocate*, I (June, 1957), 80–83.

HILLERBRAND, HANS J. "Dietrich Bonhoeffer and America," *Religion in Life*, XXX (Autumn, 1961), 568–79.

HUDNUT, W. H. "Reply" (to Berger). *The Christian Century*, LXXVI (May 20, 1959), 618–19.

JENKINS, DANIEL. *Beyond Religion*. Philadelphia: Westminster Press, 1962.

KOOPS, H. A. "Ethics of Dietrich Bonhoeffer and Crisis of Nuclear Power," *Reformed Review*, XIX (September, 1965), 25–39.

LEHMANN, PAUL L. "Commentary: Dietrich Bonhoeffer in America," *Religion in Life*, XXX (Autumn, 1961), 616–18.

LEIBHOLZ, S. B. "Dietrich Bonhoeffer; a Glimpse into our Childhood," *Union Seminary Quarterly Review*, XX (May, 1965), 319–31.

LEVI, A. "Bonhoeffer and Delp: Papers from Prison," *Month*, XXXI (June, 1964), 328–36.

LILLIE, W. "Worldliness of Christianity," *Expository Times*, LXXV (February, 1964), 132–37.

LOCKMAN, J. M. "From the Church to the World," in *New Theology No. 1*, edited by M. E. Marty and D. G. Peerman. New York: Macmillan Co., 1964. Pp. 169–81.

LOEFFLER, P. "Bonhoeffer versus Congar," *Frontier*, VII (Summer, 1964), 130–33.

MARK, JAMES. "The Last Thoughts of Dietrich Bonhoeffer," *Quarterly Review of the Community of the Resurrection*, No. 240 (1963), 11–14.

MARKUS, R. A. "Relevant Pattern of Holiness, Dietrich Bonhoeffer's Ethics," *Hibbert Journal*, LV (July, 1957), 387–92.

MARLÉ, RENÉ S. J. "Bonhoeffer: The Exigency of His Message," *Continuum*, IV, No. 1.

MARTY, MARTIN E. "Bonhoeffer: Seminarians', Theologian," *The Christian Century*, LXXVII (April 20, 1960), 467–69.

MEHTA, V. "Profiles," *New Yorker*, XLI (November 27, 1965), 65–68+.

MINTHE, ECKHARD. "Bonhoeffer's Influence in Germany," *The Andover Newton Quarterly*, New Series, II (September, 1961), 13–45.

NIEBUHR, REINHOLD. "The Death of a Martyr," *Christianity and Crisis*, V (June 25, 1945), 6–7.

OGLETREE, THOMAS W. "The Church's Mission to the World in the Theology of Dietrich Bonhoeffer," *Encounter*, XXV (1964), 457–69.

PHILLIPS, JOHN A. "Dietrich Bonhoeffer: the Letters and the Legacy," *Motive*, XXVII (February, 1967), 39–44.

RIDD, J. C. "Message from Bonhoeffer," *The Christian Century*, LXXXIII (June 29, 1966), 827–29.

ROBINSON, J. A. T. *Honest to God*. Philadelphia: Westminster Press, 1963.

RUNIA, K. "Dietrich Bonhoeffer: The Man and His Beliefs," *Eternity*, XVI (December, 1965), 11–13+.

SCHNEIDER, EDWARD D. "Bonhoeffer and a Secular Theology," *Lutheran Quarterly*, XV (1963), 151–57.

SCHWARZCHILD, S. S. "Reply" (to Cox). *Commonweal*, LXXXIII (November 26, 1965), 227+.

SHERMAN, FRANKLIN. "Dietrich Bonhoeffer," in *A Handbook of Christian Theologians*, edited by D. G. Peerman and M. E. Marty. Cleveland: World Publishing Co., 1965. Pp. 464–84.

————. "Death of a Modern Martyr; the Witness of Dietrich Bonhoeffer," *Expository Times*, LXXVI (April, 1965), 204–7.

SHINN, R. L. "Dietrich Bonhoeffer: 1906–1945," *Christianity and Crisis*, XXV (April 19, 1965), 75.

SMITH, RONALD GREGOR. *The New Man.* New York: Harper & Row, 1956.

————. *Secular Christianity.* New York: Harper & Row, 1967.

VAN BUREN, PAUL M. *The Secular Meaning of the Gospel.* New York: Macmillan, 1963.

VAN DEN HEUVEL, A. H. "Secularization as Freedom and Yoke," *Study Encounter*, I, No. 2 (1965), 55–63.

VISSER 'T HOOFT, W. A. "Dietrich Bonhoeffer: 1945–1965," *Ecumenical Review*, XVII (July, 1965), 224–31.

WEBER, H. "Worldly Holiness," *Frontier*, I (January, 1958), 19.

WEDEL, T. O. "Man Come of Age," *Union Seminary Quarterly Review*, XVIII (March, 1963), 326–40.

WENTZ, F. K. "Lay Renaissance: Europe and America," *The Christian Century*, LXXVI (May 13, 1959), 576–79.

WESSON, ANTHONY J. "Bonhoeffer's use of 'religion'," *The London Quarterly and Holborn Review*, January, 1967, pp. 43–53.

WEST, CHARLES C. "Dietrich Bonhoeffer—the Theologian," *The Student Movement*, LVI, No. 3 (1954), 27–29. The same article appeared in *Campus Lutheran*, VI (December, 1954), 23–25.

(Unsigned). "Bonhoeffer: Representative Christian," *The Christian Century*, LXXXII (April 7, 1965), 420–21.

(Unsigned). "Theologian of Life," *Time*, LXXV (May 9, 1960), 53–54.

CONTRIBUTORS

JOHN C. BENNETT—President and Reinhold Niebuhr Professor of Social Ethics, Union Theological Seminary, New York, New York.

PAUL M. VAN BUREN—Professor of Religion, Temple University, Philadelphia, Pennsylvania.

PAUL L. LEHMANN—Auburn Professor of Systematic Theology, Union Theological Seminary, New York, New York.

EBERHARD BETHGE—Rector of the Pastoral College of the Rhineland, Rengsdorf, Germany and Harry Emerson Fosdick Visiting Professor (1966–67) at Union Theological Seminary, New York, New York.

MARIA VON WEDEMEYER-WELLER—Bonhoeffer's fiancée at the time of his death and the recipient of more than forty prison letters, many of which were written later than those published in *Letters and Papers from Prison*. Mrs. von Wedemeyer-Weller, now residing in the United States, has not appeared in print before.

JOHN D. GODSEY—Professor of Systematic Theology, The Theological School, Drew University, Madison, New Jersey.

PETER VORKINK, II—Book Review Editor, *Union Seminary Quarterly Review*, New York, New York.